Enduring Wisdom for
Today's Spiritual Seekers

154 Provocative Questions for Everyday Life
...with Insightful Guidance from the Gospels

James J. Bacik
RC Priest

Univ. Toledo Prof, 40 yrs.

RC

Enduring Wisdom for Spiritual Seekers

154 Provocative Questions for Everyday Life
…with Insightful Guidance from the Gospels

Text copyright © 2019 by James J. Bacik *84 yrs. dd*

Cover design and typesetting by Courter & Company
Cover image by Alewiena_design / Shutterstock.com

Published by ACTA Publications, 4848 N. Clark Street,
Chicago, IL 60640, www.actapublications.com

Library of Congress Catalog Number: 2019933597

ISBN: 978-0-87946-667-1

Printed in the USA by Total Printing Systems

Year 30 29 28 27 26 25 24 23 22 21 20 19

Printing 15 14 13 12 11 10 9 8 7 6 5 4 3 2

Text printed on 30% post-consumer recycled paper.

For Robert A. Holden

—

My good friend who made vacations fun and golf challenging.

My brother priest who was an outstanding pastor and
authentic servant leader.

My spiritual director who offered solid practical advice.

My Enduring Sign of Hope who has continued for over 50 years to
manifest the fruits of an early life-changing encounter with
the Gracious Mystery.

Contents

—

FOREWORD BY BERNARD (BOB) BONNET — 11
Executive Director, Association of U.S. Catholic Priests

INTRODUCTION — 15

CHAPTER ONE — 23
Christian Anthropology (analyzing Human Existence):
Individual Perspectives

How do I feel about the future?
How can I stay centered in my busy life?
Do I suffer from spiritual paralysis?
How can I make better use of my resources?
What are my most troublesome blind spots?
Am I in the habit of comparing myself to others?
In what ways am I hearing impaired?
How can I draw on my faith more effectively?
Do I find spiritual nourishment in shared meals?
Do I feel called to take up the cross?
Am I guilty of complacency?
Do I tend to take blessings for granted?
How do I manage my money?
Am I able to accept my limitations?
Am I tempted to take the easy way out?
Am I in danger of neglecting my spiritual life?
Am I influenced by consumerism?
What role does fasting play in my life?
How generous am I?
Is procrastination a problem for me?
Do I have a healthy outlook on sexuality?
How can I survive tragedies?
Do my actions match my beliefs?
Am I constructively self-critical?
Am I prepared for death?

Chapter Two — 63
Christian Anthropology (analyzing Human Existence):
Social Perspectives

How can I manage relational conflicts?
Does my faith affect my family relationships?
Am I ready to forgive my relatives?
Am I guilty of prejudice and intolerance?
Am I tempted to religious exclusivism?
Am I grateful for God's forgiveness?
Am I tempted to exalt myself over others?
Are there limits to my willingness to forgive?
Am I open to reconciling strained relationships?
Am I overly concerned with impressing others?
Do I tend to hold grudges?
Do I see myself as superior to others?
Am I open to truth and goodness whenever it appears?
Am I too controlling in my relationships?
What is my vision of an ideal marriage?
Do I treat others as equals?
Am I guilty of stereotyping others?
How can I act more like a Good Samaritan?
How seriously do I take the law of love?
What can I learn from the Prodigal Son?
Do I really try to love my enemies?
Am I able to accept my limitations?
How can I improve my friendships?
Am I satisfied with my community involvement?
How do I relate to my deceased loved ones?

Chapter Three — 101
The Doctrine of God (reflecting on the Gracious Mystery)

Am I too busy to pray and rest?
How can I find joy in life?
Is my relationship to God influenced by marketplace values?
What is the relationship between my image of God and my self-image?
What can I learn by reflecting on the Trinity?
How can I take better advantage of life's opportunities?

How can I overcome anxiety and multiply my talents?
How can I best prepare for the future?
How can I better manage my fears?
How can I become a more trusting person?
What are my top priorities?
Am I in danger of putting God to the test?
Am I bothered by guilt feelings?
What role does the Holy Spirit play in my life?
How do I handle the little deaths of life?
Do I feel threatened by the evil in the world?
How receptive am I to the Word of God?
Do I appreciate the depth dimension of everyday life?
Am I aware of signs of hope in my life?
What are my own deepest spiritual experiences?
How can I find peace when my soul is troubled?
What does the Lord's Prayer mean to me?
How important is God's kingdom in my life?
Which person of the Trinity is most important to me?

Chapter Four — 139
Christology (following Jesus, Our Friend)

Who is Christ for me?
How can I become a more compassionate person?
Where can I find light in the midst of darkness?
Am I attuned to the voice of the Good Shepherd?
Do I honor Christ as my king?
Am I ever amazed by Christ's grace?
Where can I find help to bear the burdens of life?
Am I open to the healing power of Christ?
How do I deal with my personal demons?
Where do I find joy in my life?
Do I have faith in the healing power of Christ?
Am I prepared to meet Christ in my life?
How can I manage the storms of life?
What are my most intense spiritual hungers?
How does the Eucharist nourish my soul?
Do I accept Christ as my king?
Am I committed to Christ?

What role does the resurrection play in my spiritual life?
What does it mean to me to follow Christ?
Where can I find mercy and forgiveness?
Am I ready to take up the cross to follow Christ?
How do I relate to Christ the Liberator?
Where can I find wisdom for life?
How can I be more open to Christ's forgiveness?
Do I accept Jesus as Lord of the Sabbath?
How can I share more deeply in the life of Christ?
Do I recognize the voice of the Good Shepherd?
How can I stay alive spiritually?
What does it mean to participate in the Paschal Mystery?

Chapter Five — 181

Ecclesiology (forming the People of God)

Do I recognize Christ in the breaking of the Bread?
How can Lent help me overcome my temptations?
How can I grow spiritually during Advent?
What can I learn from Luke's account of the temptations of Christ?
Do I hear the call to holiness?
How can I gain a greater appreciation of the Scriptures?
What can I learn from the Transfiguration?
What scene in Luke's Passion narrative most inspires me?
How can I make Easter Mass more spiritually enriching?
Do I experience Christ's presence at Mass?
How does the Ascension impact my spiritual life?
Where can I find energy for my spiritual life?
How can I better manage Christmas busyness?
What can I learn by reflecting on Matthew's version of the Passion?
Do I see Mary as a model of discipleship?
What spiritual guidance can I get from the man born blind?
What can I learn about faith from the Samaritan woman?
What spiritual direction does Cleopas provide?
What impresses me most about Mary of Magdala?
What does Doubting Thomas teach me about faith?
What can I learn about humility from John the Baptist?
What can I learn about discernment from Mary?
What does the Canaanite woman teach me about faith?

How does John the Baptist encourage me to persevere in doing good?
What can I learn about repentance from John the Baptist?
What advice can I glean from the story of Zacchaeus?
What can I learn about fidelity from Vaclav Maly?
What inspiration can I find in the life of Martin Luther King?
What can I learn about faith from Karl Rahner?

Chapter Six — 225
Christian Life (living the Gospel)

Am I comfortable witnessing to my faith?
How can I participate more fully in the mission of Christ, the Suffering Servant?
How can I become a more faithful citizen?
How can I cooperate more effectively with the Spirit?
How can I keep a healthy perspective on evil in the world?
Am I tempted to rash behavior?
Am I attentive to the needs of those on the margins?
Do my actions consistent and authentic?
How seriously do I take the law of love?
Do I have escapist tendencies?
Do I feel an obligation to serve others?
How can I help the poor?
Am I tempted to self-righteousness or moral minimalism?
Am I too attached to money?
What extra baggage am I carrying?
Am I really aware of my gifts and talents?
Do I see myself participating in the mission of Christ?
How can I travel lightly and promote peace?
Do I strive for the high idealism of the beatitudes?
Do I see myself living a Christian vocation?
What could I do to foster Christian unity?
Do I recognize my responsibility to spread the Kingdom in the world?

Foreword

by Bob Bonnot, President,
Association of U.S. Catholic Priests

A merican culture is awash in varieties of spiritual thought and practice. Large numbers of people consider themselves spiritual but not religious. Varied options from atheism and Buddhism to yoga and Zen are available everywhere—online, in bookstores, in small groups, and in a variety of temples and spirituality centers. From being "a Christian nation" the United States has become an interreligious one, if truly religious at all. A 2015 Pew Research study indicated that one-third of young Americans from 18-33 are religiously dis-affiliated, although perhaps interspiritual is a better term for where our culture is today. People feel free to construct their own religious identity, often blending miscellaneous traditions in their own unique way. Gospel wisdom and Christian spirituality now function in a highly competitive market.

Christian churches of all varieties have been rocked by the tremors of tectonic movements of our planet's spiritual plates. Christianity's center of gravity has shifted from the northern hemisphere to the southern hemisphere. The stability and vitality of the Christian community in the north seems to be draining away. The number of nones (people who identify their religious affiliation as "none of the above" is growing in all generations, especially among young people born in the last thirty years. All of this raises the question of whether a Gospel-based spirituality and lifestyle can still attract and nourish the spiritual seekers of our time. Can the Catholic Church help them find in Christ and the Gospels what they are looking for? Who can provide that help? And How?

My friend and fellow-priest, Fr. Jim Bacik, does so in this timely book. A life-long spiritual seeker himself, one open to wisdom wherever he finds it, Jim has explored the vast field of religious thinking, teaching, and spirituality. He has spent most of those years deeply engaged in the intellectual and spiritual ferment of secular universities, unafraid of exploring the many currents of spirituality that have run through generations of college age youth, their parents, and their professors. He has consistently stepped beyond the campus to speak to audiences of adults trying to make contemporary sense of their Christian heritage and its richness in today's world. He has helped Catholics especially to appreciate the guidance of the Gospel and its relevance to living a Christian life, but his influence has not been limited to his own denomination or even the Christian faith.

Yet Jim's approach to both ministry and teaching is deeply rooted in the Scriptures, Catholic tradition, and Christian theology. His main mentor was one of the theological giants of the 20th century, Karl Rahner. Rahner's thought responded head-on to the human search for faith and meaning throughout the ages. While his spiritual framework was rich but complex, it was often beyond either the capacity—and/or the patience—of most seekers. What Jim Bacik has done in this book is to make Karl Rahner's theology accessible to all.

Jim has been a gift to the Diocese of Toledo Ohio, the Church in the State of Ohio, and the Church in the United States. I heard about him early on in my own priestly ministry in Youngstown, Ohio, and on many occasions experienced his down-to-earth pastoral wisdom. It wasn't until the late 1980s that I really got to know him and his charism, however. I worked with him on generating a 25-segment video series (based on Karl Rahner's Foundations of Christian Faith), which has been hailed as a challenging introduction to Christianity for college students.

Most of Jim's ministry has been as a campus chaplain in two state universities: Bowling Green and Toledo. In Toledo he was pastor of Corpus Christi University Parish, where he oversaw the design and building of a beautiful contemporary church and complex that lends itself to good liturgy, contemplative prayer, and lifelong learning. He has taught classes for university students and ran lecture series for adults throughout those years, and he is still doing so as I write. His topics are always timely, his insights practical, his spirit pastoral. Over the decades of his ministry, he has helped several generations of young people find the depth of meaning every human person needs, deserves, and seeks. Along the way he came to be esteemed as among the wisest and most successful of campus ministers nationally.

This collection of 154 mini-reflections is a jewel box of spiritual wisdom. Each essay is a gem that speaks to a particular spiritual question we all face. In just 500 or so words, Jim offers "enduring wisdom" to the many spiritual questions of our time, starting with "How do I feel about the future?" and ending with "Do I recognize my responsibility to spread the Kingdom of God?"

Each entry opens with what St. Ignatius of Loyola called a "composition of place," sketching a Gospel setting which lifts readers out of their own often confused situation into Jesus' presence. In that setting, Jim helps us ponder the question in light of Jesus' teaching and example. His short Hemingway-esque sentences using readily understandable words lead us to new insights and potential answers that invite us to consider practical responses. He then ends with a question that takes the seeker back to the search.

What I find amazing about Jim's writing is not only his ability to bring together and make sense of often puzzling Gospel passages and abstruse theological thinking but also his way of reflecting on a question in language that helps his readers "get it." Seekers both sophisticated and unsophisticated in theology will find insights here that can change their lives.

That gift constitutes a huge contribution to our times, in which the search for meaning—especially spiritual meaning—is for many anguished, confused, and without resolve. Jim's essays will speak especially to persons with a Christian background, but the Gospel stories themselves are accessible to everyone. In every instance, he offers enough examples to stir our imagination about how to become a more complete and fulfilled individual, a better and more spiritual person, and a holier and more generous Christian (should that be the path we choose to take).

Seekers longing for spiritual meaning will find their cup overflowing if they drink at this font and eat at this table.

Introduction

This book can be used in various ways. One is to take it as a sequential summary of Christian doctrine which moves logically through the major theological categories: Christian Anthropology (questions about Human Existence)—both Individual and social perspectives, The Doctrine of God (what I call the Gracious Mystery), Christology (the study of Jesus, Our Friend), Ecclesiology (the study of the People of God), and Christian Life (our work, family and friends, and community)—the sequence found in Karl Rahner's classic summary work *Foundations of Christian Faith*. All these meditations draw on Gospel passages familiar to many, taken from the *New Revised Standard Version* of the Bible. Collectively the 154 meditations provide an overview of what the Christian faith is all about. The repetition of major themes highlights the Vatican II teaching on the "hierarchy of truths," which means that some doctrines are more important than others and are worthy of repetition. These fundamental core truths provide a perspective and framework for reflecting on our more peripheral beliefs and practices.

The individual meditations are all correlational which means they all begin with a personal existential question followed by a response found in relevant Gospel passages. Starting theological reflections with a question is an effective traditional method as demonstrated by Thomas Aquinas, especially in his classic *Sum-*

ma. Furthermore, Karl Rahner's consistent effort to produce a correlational theology has enriched teaching, preaching, and pastoral practice in the contemporary Church. He insisted that the more scientific theology is the more spiritually and pastorally relevant it will be. A truly scientific theology is in touch with the significant questions of the day as well as the diverse Christian tradition. Still today, there remains a danger that theology is answering questions that no one has or that it appears abstract and out of touch with real life concerns. The meditations in this book are designed to respond to common human concerns, such as how I can maintain a consistent prayer life amidst a demanding schedule or do a better job of managing the inevitable conflicts of family life or make Christ more important in my life. In each meditation the question is in dialogue with fundamental Christian teaching based on Gospel passages. My hope is that readers who work their way sequentially through the whole book will come to a deeper realization that the Gospels do indeed have an enduring wisdom that speaks to us today.

The meditations take into account some consensus points of modern biblical criticism. The Gospels are not objective biographies but are faith documents written by believers to solidify the faith and to spread it. The evangelists were not eyewitnesses but made use of oral traditions and earlier written sources. Mark wrote first around 70 A.D. and served as a source for both Matthew and Luke, who wrote in the middle 80s. John's Gospel, based on the teachings of the Beloved Disciple, reached its final form sometime in the 90s. The Synoptics Gospels—Mark, Matthew, and Luke—have much material in common but each of the evangelists has his own theological interests and perspectives. Matthew and Luke also had a common written source, now lost, known as the "Q" document which contained sayings of Jesus, including the Lord's Prayer and his Great Sermon. The Synoptics present parables designed to promote deeper reflection on the kingdom of God. John's Gospel does not have kingdom parables but structures its treatment of the life-giving message of Jesus around seven progressively more impressive "signs," starting with turning water into wine at Cana and ending with the resuscitation of Lazarus. The second part of John contains the long farewell discourse of Jesus at the Last Supper.

From a literary perspective, we can read the Gospels as classic texts with a surplus of meaning. They are timeless narratives that can yield fresh insights when engaged by new questions. In this book, some Gospel stories are repeated as a response to diverse questions, demonstrating the inherent power of the Gospel to touch our mind and heart in various ways.

Each one of the meditations has specific examples of individuals, some famous most ordinary, who have struggled with the question or lived the Gospel response. Centuries before Christ, the Greek philosopher, Aristotle, taught us that the best way to understand a virtue is to observe a good person practicing it. Recent studies suggest that individuals find motivation for acting virtuously from others who have already done so. A wife might say if my friend forgave her wayward husband and made their marriage work, then I should at least try to forgive my husband and open up the possibility of reconciliation. Good example is a powerful motivator.

Some of the exemplary individuals who appear in these meditations are biblical figures: Mary of Nazareth, John the Baptist, Mary of Magdala, the Samaritan woman, Cleopus, Zaccheus, the man born blind. Others are public figures: Vaclav Maly, Karl Rahner, Martin Luther King, Mother Teresa. But most are ordinary believers who exemplify Gospel witness. In some cases, I simply reported their stories as I knew them. In other cases, I disguised their experiences in various ways. Many of them are composite stories which I put together from individuals known to me in diverse situations. In general, the examples are rooted in my pastoral practice extending over more than fifty years. I suppose the repetitions are due to the common character of human nature, the similarity of contemporary challenges, and the types of personal struggles brought to the confessional and the counselling room. At any rate, I know I have been inspired and energized by the good example of so many people and hope their stories can be helpful to my readers.

Those who read sequentially through the whole book can gain a concrete feel for the major themes of Christian doctrine. Drawing on Rahner's theology, we can see ourselves as self-transcendent persons with a positive orientation to the gracious Mystery we call God. As Augustine famously noted, we have "restless hearts" that can finally be satisfied only by total union with God. We remain a mystery to ourselves as we walk this earth. We are the intriguing combination of infinite longings and finite capabilities, which plays itself out in our daily lives. Chapter One, *Christian Anthropology: Individual Perspectives*, provides concrete examples of the way individuals respond to common concerns, such as How do I feel about the future? What are my most troublesome blind spots? How can I stay centered in my busy life? Do I tend to take blessings for granted? Wrestling with these kind of questions from a Gospel perspective gives us an existential sense of our self-transcendent nature.

We are not only oriented to Mystery, we are at the same time interdependent persons, who best flourish in healthy communities, starting with the family. We are social beings who actualize ourselves in and through our personal relationships. Our close relationships generate our deepest joys as well as significant challenges. Christian anthropology must have a strong social dimension to counter the isolating individualism so prevalent in our culture. The meditations in the second chapter, *Christian Anthropology: Social Perspectives* provide specific examples of how individuals have applied Gospel wisdom to the challenges of communal living: How can I manage the inevitable conflicts of family life? Am I tempted to exalt myself over others? Do I really try to love my enemies? How do I relate to my deceased loved ones?

Those who read straight through this chapter will encounter familiar challenges to communal life as well as inspiring examples of individuals who have put the law of love into practice.

In Rahner's sequence, the doctrine of God follows his theological anthropology. God is the Source of our self-transcendent spirit and the Goal of our restless hearts. We know God by reflecting on the depth dimension of the full range of human experiences. As Aquinas taught us, God always remains incomprehensible, beyond all our efforts to probe the divine essence. The Bible gives us glimpses of the way faithful people actually experience God's presence. The Gospels record the reactions of the disciples who experienced the divine presence in the words and deeds of their Master, Jesus of Nazareth. Human concerns probed in depth with Gospel guidance lead us toward a better understanding and deeper relationship with the Gracious Mystery always beyond our grasp. The questions in this chapter, *The Doctrine of God*, begin the process: Am I too busy to pray and rest? Is my relationship to God influenced by marketplace values? How can I become a more trusting person? How receptive am I to the word of God? We all can draw inspiration from the specific examples of believers who grew in their faith while wrestling with these kinds of questions. A reflective reading of this chapter could not only deepen our faith but also lead to heartfelt prayer to the God who loves us unconditionally.

The fourth chapter, *Christology*, presumes the general conclusion of the most recent critical studies that the Gospels provide us with a substantially accurate picture of the historical Jesus. After growing up in Nazareth, he began his public ministry by subjecting himself to the baptism of John. He then went about doing good: exorcising demons, curing the sick, preaching the good news, especially by parables, and spreading the reign of God. His courageous efforts to promote the cause of God and humanity drew the ire of religious and political leaders who put him to death. But God raised him to life making him life-giving spirit for all. The Gospels portray the belief of the original disciples in the resurrection of Jesus by stories of the empty tomb and distinct appearance accounts.

Christ is indeed the definitive prophet and the absolute savior. According to Rahner, Christology is the fulfillment of anthropology. Christ is not only the parable of the Father, he is also the paradigm of fully actualized humanity. With our eyes on Jesus Christ we can envision what we are called to be. The meditations in the fourth chapter lead us to Christ through a series of questions: Who is Christ for me? Where can I find light in the midst of darkness? Where can I find help to bear the burdens of life? How does Christ satisfy my spiritual hunger? Reading all the reflections in this chapter reinforces important themes in Christology, such as the essential significance of the paschal mystery, and may also suggest new ways of relating to Christ, for instance as the liberator of captives or the cosmic Lord.

For Rahner, ecclesiology is an extension of Christology. The Church is the sacrament of the risen Christ, charged with the task of keeping alive the challenging memory of Jesus and continuing his mission in the world. As Vatican II taught and Pope Francis has vigorously reinforced, the Church is the whole People of God and cannot simply be identified with the hierarchy. By virtue of baptism, all the faithful are part of the Body of Christ, sharing in his priesthood and his mission to spread the kingdom in the world. The Church is not only a community of believers; it is also a structured institution with ordained leaders, pope, bishops and priests called to serve the whole People of God. The Church has developed a body of official teachings, such as the dogma of the Trinity and modern social doctrines. The institutional Church is nourished by a rich liturgical tradition, which includes a deep sacrament sensibility centered on the Eucharist: a Church year organized around Advent and the Christmas season and around Lent and the extended celebration of Easter. The liturgical year is also punctuated by special feasts; for example, Ash Wednesday,

Palm Sunday, the Assumption and the Immaculate Conception.

The Church honors individuals who serve as outstanding witnesses to Christ including biblical saints such as Mary of Magdala and John the Baptist as well as contemporary figures like Mother Teresa and Oscar Romero. The questions in this chapter, *Ecclesiology*, invite reflection on the way we actually experience the life of the Church: do I recognize Christ in the breaking of the bread? How can I grow spiritually during Lent? What scenes in Luke's Passion most inspire me? How does the Ascension impact my spiritual life? What can I learn from John the Baptist? Christians who read this chapter will not find a coherent ecclesiology but will be reminded of the rich resources for spiritual growth available in the Church.

The Church not only builds up the body of Christ through liturgical celebrations; it also shares in the mission of Christ to spread the kingdom and to humanize the world. Those who share in the baptismal priesthood of Christ are called not only to share in the liturgy of the Eucharist but also in the liturgy of the world, serving as leaven in society. Full participation in Mass includes a missionary summons to live the faith in everyday life. Efforts to Christianize the world propel us back to Eucharistic nourishment. The questions in this last chapter, *The Christian Life*, prompt reflection on our missionary vocation, which for most of us involves our work, our family and friends, and our community and civic involvement: Am I comfortable witnessing to my faith? How can I become a more faithful citizen? How can I help the poor? Do I see myself living a Christian vocation? The numerous examples of Christian service highlighted in this chapter can challenge our complacency and suggest specific ways of getting more involved in the mission of Christ, shared by the Church to humanize the world of politics, economics and culture.

Enduring Wisdom for Today's Spiritual Seekers, which read as a whole offers a concrete sense of the practical significance of the major Christian doctrines, can also be read as a topical resource for spiritual growth. Some examples. A busy person could read one meditation each day before going to work as a way of keeping a spiritual perspective on a demanding job. Someone serious about maintaining the true meaning of Christmas could read one of the reflections in the chapter on Christology each day during Advent. A person struggling with doubts of faith could take time to read the chapter on the doctrine of God. An elderly woman suffering anxiety over her imminent death could look through the Table of Contents and read the meditation titled: How to prepare for death? An affluent Christian searching for ways to help those in need could examine the chapter on *Christian Life* for meditations that might be helpful. A person who read this introduction and wondered who Karl Rahner is could find his name in the table of contents and learn at least a little about him.

Whether individuals read the book sequentially or topically as a spiritual resource, my hope is that the questions will resonate with the real-life concerns of the reader, that familiar Gospel passages will come alive in fresh ways, and that the many specific examples will provide insight and inspiration for those on a spiritual quest.

Chapter One

Christian Anthropology
(analyzing Human Existence):

Individual Perspectives

1. How do I feel about the future?

In Luke's Gospel, Jesus declares to the Jews that their beautiful Temple will be destroyed. The people want to know when this will happen, but Jesus tells them they should not follow false prophets who claim to know when and should not be terrified by wars and insurrections. He goes on to invoke traditional signs of the end times, such as earthquakes, famines and plagues. Warning his followers that they will suffer persecution because of his name, Jesus assures them that he will guide them and protect them from ultimate destruction. He concludes his teaching with an admonition: "By your perseverance you will secure your lives" (Luke 21: 5-19).

At the time of Jesus, there was an expectation among some Jews that God would intervene in a decisive way to free his people from the oppression of Roman rule. This expectation was expressed in what is called "apocalyptic" writings that employed vivid cosmic images to set the stage for God's saving action. The real purpose of apocalyptic literature was not to frighten people but to give them hope. Apocalyptic imagery should not be taken literally, nor does it contain clues as to when the end-time will come.

The passage reflects the apocalyptic expectations of the first century of the Christian era. Although a few Christians today expect the end of the world to come soon, most Christians are not personally engaged by this expectation. However, we all have to deal with the unknown future which awaits us. Some are overly anxious about the dangers that lie ahead while others are too complacent, failing to plan or prepare for the inevitable and the unknown. Luke reminds us both to disregard Christians who claim to know when the world is going to end and to persevere on the journey into the future with confidence in God's promise and Christ's guidance.

We can imagine Christians who have effectively appropriated various aspects of this message. A grandmother who suffers from excessive fear of damnation gradually learns to trust God's mercy, enabling her to live her last years with greater peace of mind and heart. A Catholic collegian recruited by a fundamentalist Christian group on campus talks to his pastor, who helps him see that apocalyptic passages in the Bible should not be taken literally. A bachelor who lives a carefree life starts taking seriously his responsibility to prepare financially and spiritually for old age and death.

> What is the next step I could take to prepare better for the unknown future?

2. How can I stay centered in my busy life?

In Luke's Gospel, Martha welcomes Jesus into her home and is busy providing hospitality for him while her sister Mary sits at the Lord's feet listening to him. Upset with this situation, Martha wants Jesus to tell Mary to help with the serving. Jesus replies: "Martha, Martha, you are anxious and worried about many things. There is need of only one thing. Mary has chosen the better part and it will not be taken from her" (Luke 10: 38-42).

Christians today hear this story in some questionable ways. A sister who identifies with Mary feels affirmed in her self-righteous conviction that she has chosen the superior vocation by living the vows in a religious community. A busy mother of four kids, who identifies with Martha, interprets the words of Jesus as somehow demeaning her chosen life as a wife and mother.

Accepting the scholarly view that the gospel does not favor the contemplative life over the active life, let us reflect on what Christ is telling those of us who identify with Martha and her frustration over being unfairly burdened with work. As the Gospel suggests, the Martha problem is not solved simply by reducing the workload. Jesus does not tell Mary to pitch in with the domestic chores. He does indicate that we can best deal with work related anxiety by adopting the perspective of the disciple who reflects on his words. This might mean: making persons more important than completing tasks; seeing work as a way of extending the kingdom; maintaining a contemplative spirit in the midst of demanding activities; staying calm and centered despite stressful demands; doing all for the glory of God.

We can imagine individuals responding positively to this Gospel. A wife long frustrated by her husband's adamant refusal to share in household work comes to accept this reality and with a calmer heart offers up her daily tasks as a prayer for the good of her family. A bricklayer who is forced to work with a much slower partner learns to manage his understandable frustrations by thinking of his own work as building God's kingdom on earth. A busy executive having trouble dealing with stress starts doing ten minutes of reflective prayer each morning which keeps him calmer throughout the day.

> What next step can I take to develop a more contemplative spirit?

3. Do I suffer from spiritual paralysis?

Mark tells us the fascinating story of Jesus curing a paralyzed man. Back at his home in Capernaum, Jesus is preaching the word to a large overflow crowd that blocks the door. Four men carrying a paralytic on a mat open up the roof and lower him down in front of Jesus. Seeing their faith, Jesus says to the man: "Son, your sins are forgiven." Some scribes were sitting there thinking Jesus is blaspheming since only God can forgive sins. Knowing their thoughts, Jesus backs up his claim to forgive sins by curing the paralytic, who picks up his mat and walks away, much to the astonishment of the crowd that says: "We have never seen anything like this" (Mark 2: 1-12).

Don, a good friend of mine, suffered from Lou Gehrig's disease for 17 years before succumbing to this debilitating illness. Before being diagnosed, Don served the Diocese of Toledo, doing outstanding work on behalf of lay ministry. As paralysis gradually took him over, he continued to find creative ways of ministering to others. He helped out with periodic retreats at a nearby prison and tutored students in reading. He formed a small group of men who met monthly in his home to discuss their Catholic faith and their distinctive approaches to spirituality. Don attended Mass regularly throughout his illness, sitting in a wheelchair in the back of church. As I processed in for Mass, we would exchange a handshake that felt to me like a personal blessing from a man who lived the paschal mystery we were about to celebrate together.

I was privileged to know something of his spiritual journey. Don understood the Gospel that celebrates Jesus as the Divine Physician who heals the soul and the body. He also came to accept and appreciate the necessary assistance provided by his wife and adult children, his friends, and his professional caregivers. His dependence on others expressed and solidified his total dependence on God. He constantly nourished his soul by reading classic and contemporary spiritual authors, and later by listening to tapes. He did not pray for or expect a physical cure, but he experienced the healing power of Christ. Don had one especially powerful mystical encounter with Christ mediated by a bus driver, who showed up—unsummoned and unexpected—and drove him home from a doctor's appointment. Near the end of his life, when he was still conscious, I celebrated with Don the Anointing of the Sick with his family and friends. People used the occasion to express their gratitude for his life and ministry. Many of us still draw inspiration from our deceased friend as we deal with our own paralyzing diminishments and endeavor to tap the healing power of the risen Christ.

> Who inspires me to deal with the paralyzing factors in my own life?

4. How can I make better use of my resources?

In John's version of the feeding of the multitude, Jesus asks Philip where they can buy enough food to feed the large crowd that was coming to him. Philip replies, in essence, that they do not have enough money to buy even a little food for each one. Andrew chimes in that a boy there has five barley loaves and two fish, but what good are these for so many. Jesus then takes the loaves, gives thanks and distributes them, and also shares the fish. After the crowd ate as much as they wanted, Jesus has the disciples gather up the leftovers filling twelve wicker baskets. Seeing the sign Jesus did, the crowd identifies him as the Prophet who is to come and wants to make him king. But Jesus withdraws to the mountain alone (John 6: 1-15).

Perhaps we could let this remarkable sign prompt reflection on two different approaches to the challenges of life. One is represented by Philip and Andrew, who are focused on what they do not have: not enough money and not enough food. Some of us may find ourselves adopting this "not enough" approach, focused on what we don't have. I don't have enough time for prayer in my busy schedule. I don't have the energy to exercise regularly. I don't know enough to vote intelligently. I don't have enough inner strength to forgive her. I don't have enough faith to overcome my doubts. Recognizing limitations can be a healthy response to the realities of life, but an excessive concentration on what we do not have can be self-limiting: curtailing creativity; settling for mediocrity; missing opportunities; underestimating the power of God's grace.

Jesus instructs us in another approach to life. He focuses not on what they don't have but on what they do have: five loaves and two fish, which ends up feeding thousands of people. The suggestion is that we can grow spiritually and be more effective disciples by concentrating less on what we do not have and more on the resources at our disposal.

We can imagine individuals rising above their limitations and following Christ's example. A plumber working a lot of overtime still finds time to pray each day. A senior citizen with limited energy still does his doctor-recommended exercise routine each day. A divorced woman, cooperating with God's grace, forgives her self-centered ex-husband. A grad student votes for the first time after reading an abridged version of the American bishops' *Faithful Citizenship*. A teacher with many doubts about Church doctrines remains a faithful Christian disciple by drawing on her core conviction that Jesus is the parable of the Father and the exemplar of full humanity.

What specific resources do I have that can help me be a more committed and effective follower of Christ?

5. What are my most troublesome blind spots?

Mark invites us to reflect on the story of a blind man with great faith by the name of Bartimaeus (Mark 10: 46-52). He is sitting by the roadside with his cloak spread out to receive alms, the only way he had to support himself. Hearing that Jesus is passing by, he cries out: "Jesus, Son of David, have mercy on me," indicating that he already believes that Jesus is the long-awaited Messiah who has power to cure him. Some people in the crowd try to shut him up but he persists, eventually getting the attention of Jesus, who calls him over and asks what he wants. The blind man says: "My teacher, let me see again." Jesus responds: "Go; your faith has made you well." Immediately Bartimaeus is able to see and becomes a follower of Jesus.

Mark, along with the other three evangelists, presented the miracles of Jesus as signs that the reign of God was at hand and that the healing power of grace was at work in the world. For us today, the Bartimaeus story reminds us that the risen Christ has the power to cure our blindness whatever form it takes.

To access Christ's healing power, we need to recognize our own particular blind spots. Some possibilities: an intellectual blindness that limits our ability to see important truths about life; an emotional blindness that clouds our perceptions of the deep feelings that influence our daily moods; a moral blindness that prevents us from recognizing ethical obligations and Gospel ideals; a spiritual blindness that dulls our discernment of God's grace at work in our lives. Following the example of Bartimaeus, we need to seek the Lord's help in dealing with the specific blind spots that are retarding our spiritual growth.

We can imagine some examples of individuals seeing the light with Christ's help. A well-educated cradle Catholic, who recognizes that he is functioning with a grade school understanding of his faith, attended lectures on Catholicism sponsored by his parish. A busy mother of three, surprised to realize she no longer feels comfortable in adult settings, joins a book club which involved her in serious discussions with other women. A factory worker, who recognizes that he is reflexively tuning out Pope Francis on climate change, reads the pope's encyclical on the environment. A school teacher pondering the example of Bartimaeus identifies a spiritual blind spot that kept her from seeing Christ in a couple of her work colleagues, prompting her to be more attentive to their good qualities.

How could I be more opxen to Christ's healing power?

6. Am I in the habit of comparing myself to others?

In Matthew's Gospel, we find the parable about the workers who labored all day in a hot sun grumbling against the landowner because he paid guys who worked only one hour the same daily wage that they received (Matthew 20: 1-16). We can understand their displeasure. The arrangement seems to violate our sense of justice or fair play. Common sense says those who worked longer hours should get paid more money. The owner, however, responds that he paid them a just, agreed-upon wage, and then adds the insightful suggestion that their real problem is that they are envious because he was so generous to the other workers.

This parable can move us to deeper reflection on our fundamental attitudes about life. Envy, traditionally considered one of the seven capital sins, inclines us to be sad over the good fortune of others. It is rooted in a comparative mode of consciousness, which measures our own worth in terms of being better than others. Comparing ourselves unfavorably with others can lead to poor self-image and low self-esteem, while favorable comparisons can lead to pride and arrogance. If the first hired did not know that the latecomers got paid the same, they would have gone home content. Once they fell into a comparative mode, however, they became envious and lost their inner peace. If they had avoided the trap of comparative consciousness, they could have exhibited a more positive response by rejoicing in the good fortune of the workers who, after laboring for only one hour, had enough money to feed their families for another day.

The parable challenges our natural tendency to live in a comparative mode, a tendency reinforced and intensified by our competitive culture that exalts being number one. Liberated from the constraints of comparison, we are in a better position to avoid both pride and envy and to rejoice in the good fortune and accomplishments of others. For example, a man, who was always envious of his smart, good looking, accomplished older brother, comes to accept and treasure his own unique gifts and talents, thereby transforming his envy into a genuine appreciation of the ways God had blessed his brother.

A woman, who describes herself as "green with envy" towards the more affluent members of her bridge club, hears a homily that helps her recognize the root of her envy problem. She resolves to stop comparing herself to others; to cease living in a comparative mode; and to transform her comparative consciousness into accepting herself as a beloved child of God. Each morning she asks God for the gift of self-acceptance, and each evening she prayerfully reflects on any time that day she fell into the trap of comparative thinking. Over a period of time, she finds herself with greater peace of mind and a more positive attitude toward her friends, even to the point of rejoicing in their good fortune.

> How can I avoid living in a comparative mode?

7. In what ways am I hearing-impaired?

In Matthew's story of the transfiguration, Jesus takes Peter, James, and John up a high mountain and is transfigured before them. Moses and Elijah appear and then God, speaking through a cloud, says of Jesus: "This is my Son, the Beloved; with him I am well pleased; listen to him!" (Matthew 17: 1-9).

Listening to Christ, God's beloved Son, is crucial to developing a more mature Christian spirituality. We grow spiritually by becoming better hearers of the Word, more attuned to the voice of the Good Shepherd, more attentive to Christ's Spirit living within us. Christ himself is the Word of God who reveals the Father by his life and actions. He is Lord of the universe and Master of history. As risen, he is now present to all people in all cultures at all times. Through his Spirit, the whole world is graced and all things are potentially revelatory. Since Christ can speak to us in many different ways, we are wise to expand the channels of communication and to open our hearts to new ways the Lord might reach out to us.

We can learn from others who have expanded their openness to Christ. A devout grandmother, who always hoped for a clear sign from God, now hears Christ speaking to her through her grandchildren, who bring her great joy. A lawyer, who was usually too busy to smell the roses, is now attentive to the beauties of nature, leading him to prayerful praise of the Source of all beauty. A collegian, who sometimes felt embarrassed by her uneducated parents, learns to appreciate their fundamental goodness and practical wisdom rooted in their Christian faith. A factory worker, who is often upset by his self-centered, overbearing co-worker, now tries to be more tolerant and forgiving towards him. A former Catholic, who was convinced that the institutional Church has distorted the compassionate voice of Christ, is now reading everything she can find by and about Pope Francis because he sounds Christ-like to her. A retired engineer, who never listens to the hierarchy pontificating on economic issues, begins tutoring inner city grade school children and now hears the voice of Christ in the cries of the poor. A mother, overwhelmed by the death of her teenage son, responds to the voice of the Lord calling her to be strong for her other children.

On Mount Tabor, God commanded each one of us to listen to his beloved Son, who broadcasts his message through more channels than we can imagine. Our task is to become better hearers of the Word, more attentive to the many voices of Christ. Today is a good opportunity to open up at least one new neglected channel of communication with Christ: the richness of the natural world; our own healthy intuitions; the good example of others; the dark tragedies of life; a good book or movie; or a conversation with a loved one.

> What concrete step can I take today to open up deeper and broader communication with the Lord?

8. How can I draw on my faith more effectively?

Luke informs us that the apostles said to the Lord, "Increase our faith" (Luke 17: 5). They made this plea for help after Jesus taught them to care for the "little ones" and to always forgive those who offended them. Faced with such a challenging teaching, they assumed they needed more faith.

We know something about this need for an increase of faith. Individuals express their desire for more faith for various reasons: to keep functioning after the death of a wonderful spouse; to stay positive after the loss of a job; to still trust God after the suicide of a teen; to reject prejudice after another terrorist attack; to keep praying after prayers are not answered; to keep trying after many failed efforts to get over an addiction.

When the apostles asked for an increase of faith, Jesus replied: "If you had faith the size of a mustard seed, you could say to this mulberry tree, 'Be uprooted and planted in the sea,' and it would obey you." (Luke 17: 6). In his typical fashion, Jesus answered the question by suggesting a broader perspective. Faith by its very nature is a rich resource with amazing power to accomplish good. It involves a fundamental openness to the all-powerful God who freely shares his divine life with us. Faith is not an autonomous possession which we can use as we wish for our own purposes. It is a gift that enables us to cooperate with God's grace and share in the divine power.

From this perspective, the challenge is not to increase our faith but to use the faith we already have to tap into the divine energy: a renewable resource always available to us. The mustard seed parable does not deny the possibility or desirability of increasing and deepening our faith, but it does invite us to begin to use the faith we have to cooperate with God's grace in doing good.

Some examples of Christians relying on this teaching of Jesus: a grieving widow keeps attending Sunday Mass and doing a daily meditation even though they bring her very little comfort, on the faith conviction that despite appearances God will not abandon her; a philosophy professor makes a conscious decision to continue to practice his Catholic faith based on his faith conviction that life does have some ultimate meaning and purpose, even though he has doubts. A middle-aged man who has been unemployed for almost a year keeps on networking and sending out resumes, not because he expects God to intervene on his behalf but because he believes God wants him to keep trying.

> What actual faith do I have that enables me to cooperate with God's grace in doing good?

9. Do I find spiritual nourishment in shared meals?

In the Gospel according to John, we find Peter, along with six other disciples, back in Galilee after the death of Jesus in Jerusalem. They are fishing the familiar sea of Tiberias but go all night without catching anything. When dawn comes, Jesus, risen but at first not recognized by them, calls to them from the shore to cast their net over the right side of their boat, where they catch 153 large fish. The unnamed "disciple whom Jesus loved" (whom we assume to be the John who is telling this story) tells Peter that the figure on shore is Jesus. Impetuous as always, Peter jumps into the water and heads for Jesus while the others drag the net ashore. Jesus then cooks some of the fish, adds some bread, and serves them breakfast. The disciples did not presume to ask Jesus any questions, because they realized that their fishing scout and breakfast host was indeed the risen Lord (John 21: 1-14).

The various appearance accounts of the risen Christ in the New Testament cannot be formed into a consistent logical narrative, free of ambiguity and contradictions. For example, some accounts have Jesus appearing first to Mary of Magdala, while in other accounts Peter and his fellow disciples encounter the Lord first. Some passages locate the appearances in Jerusalem, others in Galilee. Paul's encounter is on the road to Damascus, which is in present-day Syria. All the accounts, however, reflect the core belief of the early Christian community that God raised the crucified Jesus to a new and glorious physical life. At the same time, each of the accounts invites reflection on distinctive aspects of the ongoing presence of the risen Lord.

John's account of Jesus serving breakfast, for example, reminds us of what is called the "table fellowship" or "meal ministry" practiced by Jesus during his public life: eating with sinners at the home of Levi; being anointed during a meal at the home of Simon, the Pharisee; dining with Zacchaeus, the chief tax collector as part of his conversion process; feeding the multitude (recorded six times in the Gospels); enjoying a meal with his friends Mary and Martha; celebrating a final Passover meal with his disciples, even performing his first miracle at a wedding feast in Cana.

Our faith conviction is that we can still encounter the risen Christ today in the common experience of sharing food. Many people find that Thanksgiving, centered on the traditional family meal, has a deeper spiritual meaning than more commercialized holidays. A couple who volunteer weekly to serve the poor at a food distribution center try to see Christ in each person they serve. Despite their busy schedules, the parents of two very active teenagers begin insisting on one family meal each week (phones turned off), which improves the entire family's personal communications and produces among them a more Christ-like family spirit. A collegian enjoys going to Sunday Mass on campus, where she often finds Christ present in the assembly of her peers, in the Scriptures proclaimed and applied, and in the sharing of the consecrated bread and wine.

> Do any of these concrete examples resonate with me, and how can I be more open to the presence of Christ in my ordinary activities?

10. Do I feel called to take up the cross?

In Mark's passion account, the death of Jesus on the cross is the culmination of his life of service to others (Mark 14: 1-15, 47). He had gone about doing good, healing the sick, exorcising demons, liberating the oppressed, and challenging the abuse of power, and this cost him his life. He did not seek suffering and death, but his fidelity to his mission to spread the reign of God, "on earth as in heaven," drew the wrath of the establishment and lead to the execution of an innocent man. The cross not only definitively completed the ministry of Jesus, but it also revealed aspects of his identity: the Suffering Servant who atones for the sins of many; the Son of Man who will come with judgment on the clouds of heaven; and, most significantly, the Son of God, whom the Roman centurion alone recognized upon the death of Jesus.

Mark does not hesitate to depict the failures of the disciples during the passion. Although Jesus taught his disciples that they must take up the cross to follow him, they were not equal to the challenge when the time came. Peter, James, and John (the big three among the apostles) fell asleep after Jesus asked them to pray and keep watch. Judas betrayed him with a kiss. When Jesus was arrested, all the disciples left him and fled. Peter denied him a predicted three times when he was challenged by one of the maids of the high priest. The only ones to stay until the end were a few women and one very scared John. Despite their failures, it was these timid followers who became the courageous leaders of the early Jesus movement.

Each of the four Gospel accounts of the passion of Jesus have an inherent power to touch our hearts in distinctive ways. Mark's version invites reflection on our own often flawed efforts to follow Jesus by taking up our own cross. The good news is that we always have an opportunity to repent of our sins and become better disciples and more authentic witnesses.

We all know people who have answered the call to take up the cross as highlighted in Mark's passion. A single mother struggling to support and raise two children starts accepting her daily crosses with more grace and less complaint. A married man, blessed with a good family and economic success, does some voluntary act of self-discipline each week to prepare for the heavy crosses that may come in the future. A woman suffering from chronic pain offers her suffering each day for some cause or person featured in the daily news. A couple deeply shaken by the accidental death of their child finds some solace by offering their immense pain at Mass in union with the crucified and risen Christ. An underemployed man, long without much hope for a better job, manages his frustration better by being more attentive to the suffering of the less fortunate. A woman who had an abortion finds forgiveness and spiritual growth by simply bearing gracefully the inevitable crosses of her decision.

> What is my own most burdensome cross and how could I carry it more gracefully?

11. Am I guilty of complacency?

In Luke's Gospel, Jesus comments on two past events: Pilate murdered some Galileans during their worship, and eighteen people died from a falling tower in Jerusalem. In each case, he points out that the victims were not punished for any moral transgressions, adding to each example the same teaching: "No, I tell you; but unless you repent, you will all perish as they did." Jesus then tells them a parable about a man who wanted to cut down a fig tree that bore no fruit for three years but gave it another year after his gardener promised to give the tree special care (Luke 13: 1-9).

We can think of this passage as a warning against complacency, a reminder not to miss God given opportunities to repent and grow spiritually. We might examine ourselves on possible pockets of self-satisfaction in our own lives: accepting too easily our moral faults as just part of who we are; unconcerned about the suffering of the less fortunate; underestimating the power of our culture to undermine our Gospel values. An honest examination of our specific areas of complacency opens our hearts to the challenging message of the Gospel. As the parable suggests, God is patient with us, but we do not have unlimited time to respond to the divine call.

A husband for years simply assumes his wife would continue to put up with his periodic emotional outbursts. When he realizes this behavior is not fair to his wife and is harmful to his marriage, he seeks help and learns to control his anger, which greatly improved his marriage. A Catholic factory worker is in the habit of ignoring racist comments by his fellow workers. Recognizing that his silence contributes to the problem, he begins to look for chances to challenge racial stereotypes and say good things about African Americans. A mother is quite content with her grade-school understanding of her faith until her daughter starts asking questions about what she was learning in her high school religion class. At that point, the mother starts looking up material on topics raised by her daughter. An elderly woman wanders through her adult years without much thought about the state of her soul. When she is diagnosed with inoperable cancer, she starts a rigorous regimen of prayer and meditation to prepare herself to meet the Lord.

> What can I do to be more responsive to Christ, who calls me to repent my complacency?

12. Do I tend to take blessings for granted?

Luke tells us that Jesus, on a journey to Jerusalem, encountered ten lepers who stood at a distance crying out: "Jesus, Master, have mercy on us!" Seeing them, Jesus says: "Go and show yourselves to the priests." On the way, they were cured. One of them, a Samaritan (the outcasts of the time) returned, glorifying God and fell at the feet of Jesus, thanking him. Noting that ten were cured, Jesus asked "Were not ten made clean? But the other nine, where are they? Was none of them found to return and give praise to God except this foreigner?" And to the Samaritan he said: "Get up and go on your way; your faith has made you well." (Luke 17: 11-19).

At the time of Jesus, leprosy was a horrible isolating disease. Lepers were forced to live outside the cities and villages, separated from family and friends. When someone approached them, they were to cry out "Unclean." The cure effected by Jesus was indeed a miraculous life-renewing event for them, allowing them to rejoin their community of family and friends. Surely, an expression of gratitude to Jesus was in order. But only one, a social outcast at that, returned to give thanks; nine did not.

The story invites reflection on our own practice of the virtue of gratitude. It seems easy to take for granted many blessings: having the gift of faith; growing up in a loving family; living in a free country; having enough to eat; relating to others who receive and return our gift of love; enjoying security because of the sacrifices of police officers, firefighters, military personnel.

A collegian who appreciates his parents support but seldom expressed it starts calling them once a week, sharing news and always adding a word of thanks. A grandmother long in the habit of asking God for favors now spends more time saying prayers of gratitude for blessings received. A husband who for years took for granted the spiritual contributions of his wife to their marriage periodically goes out of his way to thank her for enriching their life together. A nurse who was in the habit of smoking since her teenage years decides to express her gratitude to God for the gift of good health by breaking the habit.

> What concrete steps could I take to develop a more consistent practice of the virtue of gratitude?

13. How do I manage my money?

Mark tells us a poignant story. A man asks Jesus what he must do to inherit eternal life. When Jesus recalls the traditional commandments given by Moses, the man says he has kept them from his youth. Looking at him with love, Jesus says: "Go, sell what you own, and give the money to the poor, and you will have treasure in heaven." At that the man "was shocked and went away grieving, for he had many possessions." Jesus used the occasion to instruct his disciples on how hard it is for the rich to enter the kingdom of God, harder than for "a camel to go through the eye of a needle." (Mark 10: 17-30).

Let us imagine some responses to this gospel when it is proclaimed at the Sunday Liturgy. In past years, Phil, a wealthy man, has reacted negatively every time to this particular story: angry that he has to listen to it being proclaimed with a self-righteous tone; guilty about not being generous enough; worried about getting to heaven. This year a deacon gave a homily that really helped Phil, pointing out that Jesus never taught that wealth in itself is bad and that his hyperbolic example of the camel did not mean that the affluent have no shot at heaven. The deacon went on to say that what you do with your money is more important than how much you have. Relieved, Phil walked out of church, committed to making a much larger contribution to his favorite charities, including United Way and the Catholic Campaign for Human Development.

Lydia, a hardworking advertising representative, heard the gospel as a challenge to think seriously about her fundamental attitudes toward wealth and possessions. After some prayerful reflection, she admitted some things she doesn't like about herself and needs to change: too much time spent checking on her stock portfolio; too driven to accumulate more possessions; too prone to buy expensive things to impress others; too worried about providing for retirement; too close to making an idol out of money. She resolved to make a systematic effort to bring her attitude more in line with the teaching of Jesus, who admonishes all of us to put our trust in God and not rely on material goods for our worth and security. Lydia decided to start by giving some of her clothing to the local St. Vincent de Paul Society and putting a two-month moratorium on shopping for new clothes.

How could I develop a more Christ-like attitude toward money, wealth, and possessions?

14. Am I able to accept my limitations?

In Luke's Gospel, John the Baptist responds to those who are wondering if he might be the Christ, the hoped-for Messiah, by sharply distinguishing himself from Jesus, who is mightier than he is and who baptizes with the Holy Spirit and fire (Luke 3: 15-16). The situation is complicated because John has already gained a large following that is impressed with his austere lifestyle in the desert and his blunt moral teaching. Furthermore, Jesus has just submitted himself to John's baptism of repentance for sin, seeming to indicate that John is the master and Jesus is his disciple. We might imagine John being tempted to retain control of the reform movement he started that was just gaining momentum under his leadership.

But the disciplined ascetic will have none of it. He knows who he is: he recognizes his limitations; he accepts his vocational role; he vacates center stage. With genuine humility, John says he is not even worthy to perform the menial task of undoing the sandals of Jesus!

We all know individuals who have made Baptist-like adjustments in their lives. Sandy was very close to her daughter as she grew up, while her husband concentrated on supporting the family. When their daughter was faced with new challenges, such as buying a car, renting an apartment, or finding a job, she naturally turned for help to her own father, who was pleased to become more a part of her life. As the father-daughter relationship grew, however, Sandy found herself vaguely resentful, somehow diminished, relegated to a secondary position. Over time, with prayer, she came to accept the new situation and was even pleased that two people she loved so much had developed such a close relationship.

Dennis loved his job as a financial consultant. He had a great relationship with his boss, a golfing buddy, who appreciated Dennis' expertise and often sought his advice. When his boss left the firm, Dennis found himself with a new female boss who ran a tight ship, maintained an impersonal leadership style, and was not particularly interested in his opinions. He grew increasingly unhappy with his situation, to the point that it was causing him daily anxiety and hurting his health. Since he had no realistic alternative job opportunities and no real chance of improving his personal relationship with his boss, he began to work at accepting his limited role at work. Over time, Dennis achieved enough acceptance so that he no longer dreaded going to work and regained some of his satisfaction in doing his job well.

> What can I learn from John the Baptist about acceptance?

15. Am I tempted to take the easy way out?

In Matthew's Gospel, Jesus, who has up to this point concentrated his ministry in Galilee, tells the disciples that he must go to Jerusalem where he will be killed (Matthew 16: 21-27). Peter privately tries to talk Jesus out of this plan, but the Lord vigorously rejects this advice, insisting that his disciples must instead take up the cross to follow him.

Peter represents our common human temptation to take the easy way out, to choose expediency over principle, to opt for pleasure over hard work. Examples are familiar: a student regularly cheats to get good grades rather than learning to study and working hard; a couple drifts along in a mediocre marriage rather than doing the hard work of dealing openly with their fundamental problems; an assembly line worker overlooks quality-control issues as long as they don't affect him; a citizen criticizes public officials but does not make the effort to get involved in a community organization; a parishioner is unhappy with her pastor but never summons the courage to speak to him. No doubt, we can all find ways that we have taken the easy way out.

Jesus turned his sharp rejection of Peter's easy-way-out strategy into a teachable moment, instructing his disciples in the way of the cross. In his own temptations, Jesus refused the easy way of turning stones into bread, while insisting instead on remaining faithful to God's will. He was clearly not a masochist seeking suffering, but he did bear gracefully the bitter frustrations that accompanied his mission: misunderstandings with his family, the people in his hometown, and his disciples; rejection by the religious leaders; and the failure of his mission to restore Israel to covenant fidelity. His fidelity to his mission took him to Jerusalem and the death that Peter had feared. Throughout his ministry, however, Jesus had chosen to do God's will rather than compromise for political or popularity purposes. His personal example reinforced his calls for his disciples to live a life of self-sacrificing love that rejects the allure of self-centered comfort. Taking up the cross means to act on principle rather than expedience, to choose what is good, right, and just rather than what is easy.

Christians who have followed the example of Christ can inspire all of us: average students who refuse to cheat, work hard, and exceed expectations; troubled couples who overcame inertia, seek help, and work at developing a satisfying marriage; individuals who overcome peer pressure and speak out against racism, sexism, and bigotry against immigrants; citizens who transform apathy into active participation in the public square; parishioners who move from passive resentment to active collaboration with parish leaders in creating a more vibrant faith community.

> How could I do a better job of taking up the cross each day?

16. Am I in danger of neglecting my spiritual life?

In Mark's Gospel, members of the Jerusalem religious establishment try to discredit Jesus publicly by pointing out that his disciples eat with ritually unclean hands, thus failing to follow "the tradition of the elders." Jesus responds by accusing his opponents of disregarding God's truly important commandments while clinging to their human traditions. Then, Jesus instructs the crowd, insisting that people are defiled not by external factors but by evil thoughts arising in the heart that lead to evil deeds. (Mark 7: 1-23).

We can hear in this Gospel passage a warning against the kind of legalism that makes Church laws more important than God's laws, that reduces the Christian life to keeping rules, that ignores Gospel ideals, that settles for minimal responses to Christ's call to discipleship. Positively, the Gospel directs our attention to our inner life, to habits of the heart that include perspectives, motives, commitments, desires, and hopes. We grow spiritually by putting on the mind of Christ, which expands our perspectives, purifies our motives, deepens our commitments, directs our desires, and grounds our hopes. In short, today's Gospel summons us to a conversion from a legalistic approach to discipleship to a wholehearted, generous following of Christ.

Let us reflect on some personal statements of conversion. "When the Church relaxed its fasting laws after Vatican II, I developed my own practices that were much more fruitful for my spiritual growth." "In the past, I used to go to Mass out of a sense of obligation, but now I actually look forward to participating in the Sunday liturgy." "When I was in high school, I went to Confession almost every week and worried a lot about being punished for my sins; now I celebrate the Sacrament of Reconciliation only once a year, during Advent, which brings me closer to the merciful Lord than my weekly listing of sins used to do." "For years I tried to avoid a disagreeable person at work, but now I am trying to understand and treat respectfully my colleague." "At one time I was against homilies at Mass on social issues, but hearing a recent homily on Pope Francis' encyclical on the environment touched my heart and has moved me to reconsider my position."

> In what concrete ways could I develop a richer, less legalistic, interior life and make a more generous response to the call of Christ?

17. Am I influenced by consumerism?

In Luke's Gospel, Jesus refuses to arbitrate a dispute between two brothers over their inheritance, but he uses the occasion to warn against greed and making an idol out of possessions. He then reinforces his point with a striking parable. A rich man who had a bountiful harvest decides to build bigger barns and is now secure for many years: he can rest, eat, drink, and be merry. But God said: "You fool! This very night your life is being demanded of you." Jesus adds this will be the fate of those "who store up treasures for themselves but are not rich toward God" (Luke 12: 13-21).

This parable does not condemn having abundant wealth, but it does raise the question of how we manage our possessions and, more radically, what attitude we take toward material goods. Jesus explicitly warns against greed or avarice, one of the seven deadly sins, which involves an excessive love of possessions while forgetting our complete dependence on God, our ultimate source of security. Our temptations to greed are intensified by the messages propagated by consumerism: personal worth is dependent on possessions; happiness flows from wealth; affluent persons are morally superior to poor people. Furthermore, consumerism blinds us to what we really want as opposed to the false desires created by advertising, for example, for example putting greater value on expensive clothes than healthy friendships.

We can think of individuals who have found ways to overcome avarice and resist consumerism. A collegian from a wealthy family goes out of her way to befriend less affluent students. A high school religion teacher includes a section on false advertising in his social justice course, designed to get students to think critically about how the electronic media can influence their fundamental attitudes. A religious brother starts living his vow of poverty as an explicit countercultural response to consumerism rather than a burden to be reluctantly borne. A woman executive refuses a lucrative promotion so she can have more time for family and friends.

> What is the most important step I could take to avoid greed and rise above consumerism?

18. What role does fasting play in my life?

Mark reports that people objected to Jesus, asking why his disciples do not fast like the disciples of John the Baptist and the Pharisees. Jesus answers that wedding guests do not fast while the bridegroom is with them, but when he is "taken away from them" they will then fast (Mark 2: 18-22).

Jesus compares the coming of the reign of God to a wedding feast, suggesting it is a time of great celebration. We can identify Jesus with the bridegroom, whose presence is a cause for celebration. While Jesus is on the earth, working to establish the kingdom, his disciples are to rejoice in his presence. When he is "taken away from them," a reference to his death, then his disciples will fast. There is a time for fasting and a time for feasting. The disciples of Jesus do not fast because he is still present and his work to establish the reign of God is cause for joyful celebration.

The Gospel prompts reflection on the role of fasting in the Christian life. Jesus himself fasted for forty days in preparation for his battle with Satan. In the early Church, Christians fasted to purify their minds for contemplating the glory of God and unite themselves with the sufferings of Christ. Today, followers of Jesus fast for various reasons: to make reparation for sins; to prepare for upcoming challenges; to participate in the Lenten preparation for Easter; to lose weight and to get in better physical shape; to live a simpler and more disciplined life; to help protect the environment; and to be in solidarity with the poor and oppressed at home and around the world.

More Christians today are making connections between fasting and social justice. Campus ministry programs all over the country sponsor the annual Fast for World Harvest designed to raise consciousness on the plight of hungry people around the globe. Some Catholics fast and contribute the money saved to the annual Catholic Campaign for Human Development, which funds self-help programs for the poor in the United States. Bread for the World, which lobbies Congress on behalf of the poor, has asked American Christians to abstain from meat three days a week, noting it takes seven pounds of grain to produce one pound of beef. Some Catholics, influenced by the public witness of the Islamic Ramadan fast, have returned to the older practice of fasting throughout the whole Lenten season, linking this discipline to another traditional practice of almsgiving. There are individuals who fast periodically to remind themselves of their obligation to assist those less fortunate. We can hope that more Christians will recognize the link between spiritual practices like fasting and the obligation to work for social justice.

Are there ways I could make fasting a more integral part of my Christian life?

19. How generous am I?

Mark's Jesus gathered his disciples in the women's court of the Temple, where people put alms into trumpet-shaped containers. Many rich people put in large sums, while a poor widow put in two small coins worth a few cents. Jesus then instructs his disciples, noting the widow put in more than all the other contributors, for they gave from their surplus wealth but she gave all she had, her whole livelihood (Mark 12: 41-44). This widow is a model of heroic virtue and generous self-giving. She is a true follower of Jesus who gave himself up to death for our salvation. Demonstrating total trust in God, the now-famous widow calls us to be more charitable persons and more dedicated disciples of Christ.

Of course, money isn't the only thing we have to be generous with. Time is sometimes even more precious, both to ourselves and to those with whom we share it. We obviously have special talents that we can share if we are willing. But there are other things as well: wisdom, support, enthusiasm, encouragement, a listening ear, a shoulder to cry on.

We can find inspiration in the well-known generous givers of our time who have practiced heroic virtues: for example, Dorothy Day, Dr. Martin Luther King, Jr., Mother Theresa, Nelson Mandela. We can also imagine ordinary individuals who respond positively to Mark's story of the widow. A corporate executive, who always thought of himself as a generous donor, calculates that he actually contributes only one percent of his total income to charities and decides to double his contributions. A wife, married to an attentive, generous husband, vows to be more responsive to his need for affection. A married couple, both active members of the parish social justice committee, commit themselves to serving meals once a week at the local food distribution center as a way of personally encountering poor persons. A single mother of three on a very tight budget decides to continue her financial support for a local shelter for abused women. A husband who found himself getting resentful for having to care for his wife with dementia prays daily for God's help and is now attending to his wife more lovingly. A single man, disappointed that he has no children of his own, dedicates himself to becoming a generous uncle to his nieces and nephews and volunteers to be a Big Brother to a couple of boys without fathers.

> What can I learn from the widow and how can I become a more generous giver?

20. Is procrastination a problem for me?

Mark tells us Jesus initiated his public ministry by announcing that the kingdom of God is at hand and by calling four fishermen to follow him: Simon and his brother Andrew, and the Zebedee sons James and John. All four immediately abandoned their livelihood and followed Jesus (Mark 1: 14-20). The key word here is "immediately."

The total, positive, and rapid response of the first disciples is striking because we all have at least some inkling of how difficult such a decision must have been. We know the temptation to procrastinate and hedge our bets when faced with a call to expand and deepen our Christian commitment. Let us reflect on common temptations. We will get more serious about spiritual growth when we are: not so busy, not so worried about finances, not so upset with our job, not so tired, not so dissatisfied with personal relationships, not so burdened by guilt, not so caught up in civic responsibilities, not so upset by scandals in the Church, not so turned off by political gridlock, not so overwhelmed by student loans. The list of excuses to ignore or deflect the call of Christ to join more fully in his mission is endless.

Wise spiritual masters advise us to prayerfully discern the

one concrete step we could take to get off dead center and make progress in the spiritual life. Thinking in terms of giant strides, quantum leaps, and marvelous conversions may work for a few, but these can be paralyzing for many of us. Better to overcome procrastination by taking a small first step toward more committed discipleship.

A guy with a drinking problem agrees to go with a friend to at least one AA meeting. A woman who knows she needs a more mature understanding of her faith signs up for a parish lecture on the fundamentals of Catholicism. A couple in a troubled marriage agrees to get an assessment by a counselor. A father who has generally neglected his collegiate daughter schedules a lunch with her to talk over their relationship. A grad student who is always frenzied facing end of the semester deadlines starts an important paper early in the semester. A parishioner who wants to get more out of the liturgy of the word experiments with saying a short prayer as he stands for the Gospel. A successful corporate executive, long resistant to the social dimension of the Gospel, volunteers to help out at a food distribution center supported by her parish. A cynical citizen turned off by the political process determines to get back to voting intelligently in the next election. A wife who knows she should apologize to a friend tells her husband to remind her to make the call. First steps can often open our hearts to further calls from Christ.

> Are there ways I am resisting the call to deeper discipleship, and what next step could I take to participate more fully in Christ's mission?

21. Do I have a healthy outlook on sex and sexuality?

There is greater awareness these days of the hookup culture on college campuses that promotes casual sex without traditional dating, romantic gestures, or even minimal commitment. In this view, having sex is a way of satisfying physical urges without incurring any long-term obligations, as long as it is consensual and not forced. Casual sex is made possible by readily available contraceptive measures. It is justified by the general principle that sex is an autonomous possession to be used as willed for one's own pleasure and satisfaction, and it is encouraged by the common conviction that the more sexual experience the better. Although we tend to locate the hookup culture on college campuses, its fundamental perspectives and attitudes can be found throughout society, supporting premarital sex, adultery, and divorce.

In Matthew's Gospel, Jesus cites the traditional commandment forbidding adultery and adds: "But I say to you that everyone who looks at a woman with lust has already committed adultery with her in his heart"(Matthew 5: 27-30). Looking deeper, Christianity offers an alternative outlook on human sexuality that challenges the assumptions of the hookup culture. Sex is not an autonomous possession but a beautiful gift of God to be used responsibly in accord with the divine plan. Sexual expression should match and express personal commitment as it gradually deepens. The public commitment made in marriage provides the best context for developing a satisfying and fruitful sexual relationship. Casual sex divorced from romantic love and genuine commitment often proves to be empty and meaningless, as commonly reported by those involved. Wholehearted commitment to a marriage encourages couples to work through problems rather than seek a quick and easy solution in divorce. The virtue of fidelity strengthens spouses to resist the many temptations to adultery in our mobile and open society. A stable marriage provides couples with a variety of opportunities to help each other become better persons. Deepening sexual intimacy within marriage is a better path to personal development than multiplying sexual experiences outside marriage. The law of love is a more reliable and comprehensive moral principle to guide sexual activity than mutual consent. Responsible sex offers better guidance than safe sex in avoiding pregnancy and diseases. In sum, sexuality finds deeper meaning in the context of loving, committed and faithful relationships than in casual encounters.

As a challenge to hookup attitudes, Christianity offers not a series of negative prohibitions but a wisdom not of this world but from God that leads to maturity. This wisdom insists that human sexuality is a gift from God to be used responsibly for propagating children and fostering mutual love.

> How could my Christian faith exercise greater influence on my attitude toward sexuality?

22. How can I survive tragedies?

In Luke's Gospel we find dire warnings from Jesus: "People will faint from fear and foreboding of what is coming upon the world, for the powers of the heavens will be shaken." "on earth nations will be in dismay" (Luke 21: 25-28). This striking imagery pointing to the end times can also direct our attention to life as we know it now. Frightening things happen: terrorists kill innocent people; random violence strikes our cities and schools; marriages collapse; friendships break up; illness attacks healthy bodies; natural disasters disrupt life.

Christ has more positive advice for us when things fall apart: "be on guard so that day does not catch you unexpectedly." "Be alert at all times, praying that you may have the strength to escape all these things that will take place, and to stand before the Son of Man" confident that the Son of Man will one day come to restore all things in himself (Luke 21: 34-36).

We can imagine individuals who have followed the advice of the Lord when their lives unraveled. When Tim lost his job in his early fifties, he spent too much time sitting around feeling sorry for himself and anesthetizing his pain with excessive amounts of Scotch. Throughout, he wisely kept going to Mass, and one Sunday he caught part of the homily suggesting that Advent is a season of hope, a time to stay alert to new possibilities. Right then he decided to stop drinking and go to A.A., and he started making contacts to find a new job. Nothing broke his way for months, but he persevered in his networking efforts, somehow trusting that Christ was with him. When he finally found a good job, he vowed to try to help others facing similar problems.

When Rebecca's husband suddenly walked out on her after 20 years of marriage, she retreated into an inner circle of pain, anger, and frustration focused on a burning desire to get back at him. She stopped going to Mass but did continue her lifelong habit of saying prayers before going to bed. One night, while saying the Our Father, she was struck by the part about forgiving "those who trespass against us." It became clear to her that she had to forgive her husband if she was going to get on with her life. Trying to forgive proved to be a difficult process. She prayed regularly for God's help. She tried to be vigilant, blocking out negative feelings, and to stand erect, rising above her confining circle of resentment. Over time she made progress which deepened her trust in Christ, the Son of Man who restores all things.

> What collapses and breakdowns have troubled me the most and how can I manage them better with Christ's help?

23. Do my actions match my beliefs?

Matthew's Jesus says to his disciples: "Not everyone who says to me, 'Lord, Lord,' will enter the kingdom of heaven, but only the one who does the will of my Father in heaven" (Matthew 7: 21-27). Jesus goes on to reinforce his fundamental point with a parable comparing a wise man who built his house on rock so that it withstood floods and winds and a foolish man who built his house on sand so that it collapsed during a storm. The wise man is like the believer who listens to the words of Jesus and acts on them, while the foolish man is like the person who hears Christ's words but fails to act on them.

The message is clear. As Christians we are called not only to pray to the Lord but to live out his command to love our neighbor. Our ideal is a consistent living faith that preserves an organic unity between word and deed. We recognize the hypocrisy of acting in a way that contradicts our verbal commitments. We learn to trust people who keep their word. Children are more likely to become authentic Christians if they learn from their parent's example as well as their words.

Let us set up two broadly drawn scenarios of how two sets of parents might initially deal with their homosexual sons. In emotionally charged encounters, the collegiate sons from both families announce they are gay. Both have been wrestling with their sexual orientation for a few years and have already come out to close friends. Both sets of parents are from traditional religious families. None of their relatives have ever openly acknowledged a same sex orientation. In each encounter the father responds first. One of them speaks hurtful words quickly and emotionally: "Are you sure? You haven't told anyone, have you? You need a girlfriend. I heard you can fix this. I will pay for someone to help you. What will I tell my friends? Get this straightened out before you come home next month." We can hope that over time this father will come around and accept his son, perhaps encouraged by his wife and informed by a better understanding of sexual orientation. But his instant response reflects a disconnect between his commitment to Gospel values of love and tolerance on the one hand and his harsh treatment of his son on the other.

The other father responds lovingly and thoughtfully: "Son, we are pleased you initiated this conversation. Your mother and I will

57

always love and support you. We want to hear more about what brought you to this moment. I imagine you are on a challenging journey, given our homophobic culture. We will be with you every step of the way. Knowing you, I am sure you have thought this through carefully and asked God for guidance. You can count on our prayers and any help you need and want as you find your own way in life." These parents demonstrate a consistent Christian response that reflected their commitment to Christ, who calls us to love, respect and accept others in their uniqueness.

> How can I live a more consistent Christian life of action, not just words?

24. Am I constructively self-critical?

In Luke's Gospel, Jesus asks: "Why do you see the speck in your neighbor's eye, but do not notice the log in your own eye?" He has harsh words for those who act without realizing this discrepancy: "You hypocrite, first take the log out of your own eye, and then you will see clearly to take the speck out of your neighbor's eye" (Luke 6: 39-46).

Jesus is directing our attention to a common human tendency to notice the faults of others while ignoring our own. On the one hand, we know the temptation to be overly critical of others: to view them in the worst light; to exaggerate their faults; to impugn their motives; to neglect their virtues, to minimize their accomplishments. On the other hand, we are not immune from self-delusions; unable to recognize and admit limitations, vices, and sins; unaware of subtle forms of bias and prejudice; dismissive of prophetic protest against false consciousness and social sin; unable to identify rationalizations; inattentive to the spiritual dimension of life, including our own shadow side. When self-criticism is absent or underdeveloped, it is hard to see the beam in our own eye and much easier to spot the splinter in the eyes of others.

The Catholic priest and moral theologian Charles Curran provides us with a good example of the importance of self-criticism in the Christian life. Some years ago, Fr. Curran wrote an article describing his personal awakening to the problem of racism and white privilege in the United States. As a professor at Catholic University, he went out of his way to encourage the African–American women working on their doctorates. He felt at ease with his efforts to combat racism in our society. But, as he has confessed, he was "blithely unaware of how white privilege" shaped his work as a moral theologian. He simply assumed that his white theological perspective was normative, that his privileged standpoint put him in a position to judge others and make the less fortunate the object of his goodwill.

With the help of black theologians and others, Curran gradually came to recognize the bias built into his approach. He began to see how privileged he was as a white male in practically every aspect of his life, for example, attending good schools with excellent teachers—a privilege denied to many people of color. Curran began to recognize that white privilege often comes at the expense of minorities, helping create the social sin of racism.

Realizing that his new awareness demanded conversions in his own life, Curran has tried to incorporate black perspectives into his theology. He has engaged in a mutually enriching dialogue with African-American theologians. He has listened carefully to his black students in an effort to understand their distinctive experiences. He has put renewed emphasis on the spiritual dimension of the problem of racism, including the importance of prayer in addressing it. Charles Curran exemplifies the way a healthy self-criticism can lead to constructive action on behalf of others.

> What concrete thing could I do to overcome
> my major biases?

25. Am I prepared for death?

In Matthew's Gospel, we find the parable of the ten virgins who were to welcome the bridegroom when he brought his bride to his house for the first time (Matthew 25: 1-13). The five wise women brought extra oil to light their lamps in case the bridegroom was delayed; the foolish ones did not make provision for this possibility. When the bridegroom finally comes at midnight, the foolish try to borrow oil from the wise, who send them out to buy some from the merchants. By the time the foolish women get back, the door to the house is locked and they are denied entrance. Jesus concludes the parable: "Keep awake therefore, for you know neither the day nor the hour."

The biblical scholars tell us that the parable has an eschatological character, which means it is about proper preparation for the end-time. As Christians we believe Christ will one day come again to complete his saving work. Since we do not know when this will occur, it is vital to always be prepared.

The parable may mean more to us today, however, if we think of it as an admonition to be prepared to meet Christ present in our lives here and now. We encounter the Lord not just at the end-time but in the present moment. Proper preparation enables us to seize the moment, to respond whole-heartedly to the presence of Christ in each stage of life, including the final act we call death.

When Kim was diagnosed with terminal cancer, she told her pastor: "Do not let me mess this up!" She was bound and determined to be a faithful Catholic to the end, to stay close to her wonderful husband and to be a good example to her three still young children. She was passionate about preparing well for death and actively searched for guidance on how to do so. Following the advice of her pastor, she read an article on the theology of death, which convinced her to befriend death as a free and active transition that would preserve all the good she had done and make irrevocable her choice to love God.

Kim had many intimate conversations with her husband, at times reaching a spiritual depth they had not known before. Speaking separately to each of her children, she assured them of her love and did her best to comfort them. Prayer became an even more important part of her daily routine. With great emphasis on accepting the cross, she made a general confession and accepted a penance to pray each day for an individual or group in need. Her soul was touched by a powerful celebration of the Sacrament of the Sick, which included family and friends taking turns laying hands on her and saying a personal prayer for her. Kim died peacefully, well prepared to meet Christ and join his family in heaven.

How can I better prepare for encountering Christ in my everyday life and in death?

Chapter Two

Christian Anthropology
(analyzing Human Existence):

Social Perspectives

26. How can I manage relational conflicts?

The evangelist Luke gives us a glimpse of the family life of Jesus and his parents, Joseph and Mary. Each year the family made the obligatory journey from Nazareth to Jerusalem for the week-long celebration of Passover. When Jesus was twelve, about ready to assume the religious responsibilities of a Jewish adult, he traveled with his parents to Jerusalem for the feast, but he did not return with them, choosing instead to stay and participate in the weekly informal discussions held by the Sanhedrin in the Temple. After a day's journey, Joseph and Mary, realizing Jesus was not with their relatives or friends, returned to Jerusalem and found their son in the open discussion, impressing the teachers with his questions and answers. Expressing her displeasure, Mary said: "Son, why have you done this to us?" Jesus answered: "Why were you looking for me? Did you not know that I must be in my Father's house?" Mary and Joseph did not really understand what he meant, but his mother kept pondering the whole event. For his part, Jesus returned to Nazareth and was obedient to his parents, growing in "wisdom and age and favor before God and men" (Luke 2: 41-52).

We can imagine various responses by people who meditate on this story. A collegian who sees it as a rite of passage story concludes she is still too dependent on her parents and has to take some concrete steps to achieve a healthy interdependence. A mother who is overly protective of her teenage son changes course and dedicates herself to helping him use his growing freedom wisely. A husband who wants his family life to be totally peaceful recognizes that conflict is inevitable, that it can occur without anyone really being at fault, and that it can be a stimulus for greater family harmony. A wife who grew up with an abusive father realizes that she must forgive her father if she is to be a more loving spouse and mother. A young couple just starting their own family commit themselves to handing on the faith and values they both received in their wonderful families of origin.

> How can I apply this Gospel passage to my own family life?

27. Does my faith affect my family relationships?

Mark tells us Jesus and his disciples returned home, presumably not to Nazareth but to nearby Capernaum, where he has set up a second home. When his mother, brothers, and sisters hear about this, they set out "to seize" him, because they think he is "out of his mind." At this point, the evangelist interrupts his story to report a conflict between Jesus and some scribes from Jerusalem, who charge he is possessed by an evil spirit, named "Beelzebub," who enables him to drive out other demons. Jesus counters that this charge makes no sense since a kingdom divided cannot stand. Satan would be destroying himself. Mark then goes back to the family bent on seizing Jesus. They arrive at his home but cannot get in, so they send a message asking for him. Instead of responding, he tells those sitting around him: "Here are my mother and brothers. For whoever does the will of God is my brother and sister and mother" (Mark 3: 20-35).

We can glean several points about Jesus from this gospel passage. He was popular in Galilee and had already attracted the attention of scribes in Jerusalem. Joseph, his father, was deceased by this time. His home base was now in Capernaum, from which he carried on an itinerate ministry with his disciples. His opponents recognized he was a miracle worker and an exorcist but attributed his powers to Satan. Jesus himself put great emphasis on doing the will of God, which creates spiritual bonds even more important than blood ties.

It is noteworthy that Mark does not hesitate to tell us that the family of Jesus thought he was emotionally unstable and beside himself and were determined to take charge of him, by force if necessary. Some scripture scholars suggest his family, aware of his provocative teaching and miracles, feared for his safety and wanted to bring him home. At any rate, there clearly was a serious misunderstanding in a very good family composed of well-intentioned individuals.

The experience of the Holy Family reminds us that family conflicts are inevitable. Some troubles occur because of sinful actions, bad choices, and insensitive reactions. It is possible to recognize the problem and try to fix it. A mother, for example, trying to live vicariously through her daughter could come to her senses, live her own life, and allow her daughter to find her own way. Other conflicts however, just happen. No one is at fault. There is no problem to be fixed. Such conflicts have to be accepted as part of family life, the inevitable result of imperfect human beings living in close proximity, the unavoidable result of unique personalities interacting on a daily basis. They can best be managed by prayerful acceptance, patient forbearance, and wise compromise.

A Democratic husband and Republican wife agree not to talk politics during the election cycle. A mother resolves to just put up with the new independent attitude of her daughter home on break from college, avoiding useless arguments. A father prays for wisdom in dealing with his teenage son so different from his other two children.

What could I do to heal family wounds?

28. Am I ready to forgive my relatives?

As many of us have experienced special occasions, family life can be the source of great happiness and deep joy. We recall the family stories that have shaped our identity, the encounters where love trumped selfishness, and the fun times that lifted our spirits. We can only be grateful for such great blessings and offer prayers of thanksgiving.

On the other hand, family life also has the power to inflict wounds, to generate disappointment, to cause distress. No family is perfect; all families manifest some degree of dysfunction. Not even the holy family of Joseph, Mary, and Jesus was spared the piercing sword, as Simeon foretells in Luke's Gospel, which recounts the presentation of Jesus in the Jerusalem Temple (Luke 2: 22-40). The high expectations associated with family life can sharpen the pain of the inevitable tensions, slights, and disappointments generated by the intimacy of the family circle.

Given this reality, we recall the teaching and example of Jesus, who understood the crucial role of forgiveness in human affairs. Forgiveness rules out holding grudges, seeking vengeance, and planning retaliation. Forgiveness does not mean forgetting the offense or condoning bad behavior. It does mean not identifying the offender with the bad behavior but allowing the person to begin anew with us. Only forgiveness allows us to rise above inevitable hurts so that we can build better relationships.

Applied to family life, we can envision situations where forgiveness generates new life. A single woman who always wanted to be married and have a family manages to forgive God for denying her this blessing, and this frees her to make the most of the good life she has. A husband forgives his wife's infidelity, allowing them to build a better marriage together. A wife long dissatisfied with the limitations of her husband finally forgives him for being human, which reduces her frustration and increases his self-esteem. A collegian forgives her verbally abusive father and finds new energy for doing graduate studies. A mother forgives her teenage son for lying about drug use, which encourages him to enter a rehabilitation program. A grandfather forgives his daughter for not properly disciplining her children, freeing him to enjoy some fun times with them. A wife forgives her husband for repeatedly interrupting her in conversation, which prompts him to try to be more respectful. A father who finds it very difficult to forgive his wayward son asks God for the gift of forgiveness and feels his hard heart beginning to soften.

> Is there a family member I need to forgive and how can I begin this process?

29. Am I guilty of prejudice and intolerance?

As Luke tells the story, Jesus returned to his hometown of Nazareth and spoke in the synagogue identifying himself as the Messiah. He seemed to make an initial positive impact on his neighbors, who were amazed at his appealing words. But they also asked, "Is not this Joseph's son?" – perhaps indicating some doubts about a hometown boy making such claims or wondering why he didn't work miracles for them as he did elsewhere. At any rate, Jesus went on to note that two Gentiles, a widow and a leper, received God's special help when Jewish widows and lepers did not. Terribly upset with the suggestion that God somehow favored Gentiles, his neighbors turned completely against Jesus, to the point of trying to kill him but he passed through their midst and went away (Luke 4: 21-30).

This fascinating story suggests some important things about Jesus: he lived a very ordinary life in his hometown for over thirty years; he made a big impact on people in his public life by his eloquent preaching and amazing miracles; he courageously spoke the truth people needed to hear despite personal danger; he challenged the narrow minded outlook of his own people; he was willing, when the time was right, to die for the cause of God; and he came to save all people without exception.

We could think of the Gospel as an invitation to reflect on our own temptations to exclude others, to embrace prejudice, and to display intolerance.

Jill has been very upset with terrorist attacks on the United States by Muslim extremists. She is worried about the safety of her children and grandchildren. She finds herself fearful of people who look Middle Eastern, suspicious of Muslims, and negative about Islam as a violent religion. The political rhetoric about excluding Muslims resonates with her fears. Jill confesses her feelings to a Christian friend who told her some positive things about Islam: the vast majority of the 1.6 billion Muslims in the world are opposed to violent jihadism; the Quran puts great emphasis on loving God and loving neighbor; Muslims believe in doing God's will, praying every day, fasting periodically and giving alms to the poor. She warned Jill that she was falling into Islamophobia and more generally xenophobia, which means fear of all people from other countries. Jill got the point, but the conversation with her friend did not touch her heart. However, when she reflected on Jesus and his message of inclusion, especially that he died for all people, she knew in her heart that she had to readjust her whole attitude toward Muslims. She attended a prayer service at the local mosque for the victims of terrorist attacks and made initial efforts to get to know a Muslim family in her neighborhood. The Gospel does indeed have an inherent power to transform exclusion into communion and fear into love.

> How could I do better at putting on the inclusive mind of Christ?

30. Am I tempted to religious exclusivism?

Matthew preserves for us the familiar story of the astrologers from the East who follow a star to Jerusalem, seeking to honor the newborn King of the Jews. After an audience with the jealous King Herod, who sends them to Bethlehem, they follow the star to the place where Jesus was, do him homage, and give him gifts of gold, frankincense, and myrrh. Warned in a dream not to report back to Herod, they return to their country by a different route. (Matthew 2:1-12).

Matthew composed this story in the middle-80s A.D. for a community consisting of Jews, who accepted Jesus as the Messiah, and Gentile converts, who were growing in numbers. The message was pointed. The insiders, the Jewish religious establishment in Jerusalem, did not recognize Jesus as the king but outsiders, astrologers from the East, did. God revealed the truth to the Gentiles and included them in the plan of salvation.

The early Christian community decided to accept Gentile converts without major restrictions. They came to see the Gentiles are co-heirs, members of the same mystical body and co-partners in Christ's saving work.

The story of the Magi challenges all forms of religious exclusivism that claim a monopoly on God's truth and saving grace. So much strife in our world today is fueled by religious fundamentalists who see themselves as the true believers blessed by God, while others are lost in the darkness of sin and error. As Christians we cannot presume a unique claim on God's truth nor can we look down on other religions as outside the sphere of divine love. All of us need to shed any lingering exclusivism that blinds us to the truth, goodness, and beauty in other traditions. The Second Vatican Council clearly taught that the world religions are vehicles of divine truth and grace. Christians can, therefore, participate in interfaith dialogue, hoping for a deeper understanding of revealed truth. We can collaborate with others on behalf of life, justice, and peace because we hold fundamental moral principles in common.

As Christians we believe in a universal revelation available to all people. The baby honored by the astrologers came to save the whole human family. Our commitment to Christ should make us more open to the truth and goodness in other religions and more willing to cooperate with others in pursuing the common good.

> Do I tend to exclude some individuals or groups from my circle of concern and how could I be more inclusive?

31. Am I grateful for God's forgiveness?

We find this story in Luke. Simon, a Pharisee, invites Jesus to a formal dinner at his house but did not accord him the usual signs of hospitality: water for foot washing, a kiss, anointing with oil. During the meal, a woman known to be a sinner approaches Jesus while he was reclining at table, washes his feet with her tears, wipes them with her hair, kisses them, and anoints them with ointment she brought in an alabaster flask. Simon thinks to himself that if Jesus was really a prophet he would know the woman is a sinner. Aware of what Simon is thinking, Jesus presents the parable of two debtors, suggesting that the one forgiven the largest debt loves the creditor more. After contrasting Simon's lack of hospitality with the sinful woman's generous outpouring of love, Jesus said to her: "Your sins are forgiven," adding, "Your faith has saved you; go in peace." The construction of the original Greek text indicates that the woman's repentance and forgiveness came first, which then led her to Jesus and her loving attention to him (Luke 7:36-50).

This story raises the question of the relationship between forgiveness and love. Simon represents the self-righteous and proud who do not even recognize their need for forgiveness and remain hard hearted and judgmental, unaffected by God's mercy. The woman represents those who acknowledge their sinfulness, repent of the evil done, receive God's forgiveness, and become in the process more loving persons. Honest self-examination may reveal Simon-like tendencies in our own heart: unwilling to admit a particular sin; taking divine mercy for granted; harshly judgmental of others; failing to share the gift of divine mercy with others. We also recall times when our awareness of God's forgiveness has softened our hearts and prompted acts of generous love.

Our fundamental attitude toward divine forgiveness is reflected in our human relationships where self-righteousness remains an ongoing temptation even as God calls us to be more generous lovers. Again we probably know both God-given victories in the struggle between selfishness and love as well as self-induced defeats.

Consider this example. Joe, a married man who was highly opinionated, generally selfish, and often insensitive to his wife, had an affair with his secretary. His wife finds out and is inclined to get a divorce. He asks her to give him another chance. After months of tears, reflection, and prayers, she manages to forgive him and decides to stay in the marriage. We can imagine two responses on his part. In one, he considers himself lucky, makes a few superficial changes, but continues to be his selfish, opinionated, insensitive self. In another possibility, however, Joe takes the Gospel seriously. He feels very grateful to God and his wife for a second chance. He works hard at being a loving husband, tries to respect his wife's opinions, looks for ways to compliment her, and treats her as an equal. Forgiveness does have an inherent power to lead to a more generous love.

> How can I make a more generous response to the forgiveness I have received from God and others?

32. Am I tempted to exalt myself over others?

Luke often alerts us to the meaning and purpose of the parables. In this one, Jesus is addressing those who are convinced of their own righteousness and despise everyone else. Two men, a Pharisee and a tax collector, go to the temple area to pray. The Pharisee spoke a prayer to himself thanking God that he is not greedy, dishonest, and adulterous like the tax collector and others, noting that he fasts twice a week and tithes his whole income. The tax collector, on the other hand, stood at a distance, looked to heaven, beat his breast, and prayed: "God, be merciful to me, a sinner!" Jesus then says the tax collector was justified, not the Pharisee, "for all who exalt themselves will be humbled, but all who humble themselves will be exalted" (Luke 18: 9-14).

No doubt the Pharisee was an observant Jew, even going beyond the requirements of the law. His problem was his self-righteous conviction that he had earned a position of moral superiority by virtue of his legalistic observance. This arrogant conviction blinded him to his total dependence on God and prompted him to look down upon other sinful people. The tax collector recognized his sinfulness and the power of God to forgive him. He understood that justification is a free gift of God and cannot be earned by good deeds.

We can imagine various responses to the parable. A married man recognizes the dangers in his growing emotional relationship with a female colleague, turns to God for forgiveness, goes to Confession, breaks off the relationship, and commits himself to improving his marriage. A practicing Catholic who comes to see that she is overly judgmental of her younger sister who no longer goes to Mass, decides to put more effort into understanding her sister and making the spiritual journey with her. A generous Christian who often brags about his charitable giving recognizes his arrogance and decides to make more of his charitable donations anonymously.

33. Are there limits to my willingness to forgive?

Matthew begins with Peter asking Jesus how often he must forgive his brother while proposing as many as seven times, more than double the three times commonly taught by the rabbis of the time. Jesus responds: "Not seven times, but, I tell you, seventy-seven times" indicating an unlimited readiness to forgive (Matthew 18: 21-35).

Jesus then tells a parable comparing the kingdom of heaven to a king who forgave a huge debt owed by one of his servants, who, in turn, refused to forgive a much smaller debt owed by a fellow servant. Hearing of this the master castigates the wicked servant for not sharing with another the gift of debt forgiveness he had received and hands him over to the torturers. Jesus then declares: "So my heavenly Father will also do to every one of you, if you do not forgive your brother or sister from your heart."

The Gospel invites reflection on the whole issue of forgiveness. As Pope Francis often reminds us, the all merciful God never tires of forgiving us. Our compassionate Father is always ready to let us start over again, to rise above our failures, to move beyond our sins. Our Christian calling is to share that gift of forgiveness with those who have offended us. Gratitude for divine mercy should open our hearts to the possibility of reconciliation. As Christians, we have not only the teachings of Jesus but his inspiring example of actually forgiving others, including his executioners.

Following Christ's example can be difficult. We all know something of the hard heart that wants to hang on to anger and vengeance. At times, forgiveness may seem wrong: violating self-respect; approving injustice; or enabling bad behavior. On the other hand, we know that forgiveness can halt the cycle of violence and initiate reconciliation.

A wife forgives her repentant unfaithful husband and he becomes a more compassionate, loving person. A young man becomes more self-confidant after he is finally able to forgive his verbally abusive father. A woman helps create a more peaceful worksite by forgiving an insensitive colleague and eventually befriending her. Black parents help reduce racial tensions in their community by forgiving a white police officer who shot their unarmed son.

Is there someone I need to forgive?

34. Am I open to reconciling strained relationships?

In Luke's Gospel, Jesus responds to the charge of the Pharisees and scribes that he welcomes sinners and eats with them by telling the Prodigal Son parable.

Let us reflect on the story from the viewpoint of the older son. He was upset with his younger brother because he broke social customs and shamed his father by taking his third of their inheritance and going off to a foreign land. Stories reached him that his brother was blowing his inheritance by an immoral life, including soliciting prostitutes. One day he comes in from his usual hard day of work in the fields and hears the sound of music and dancing in the house. When a servant tells him that his brother has returned and that his father has quickly arranged a big party for him, he is angry and refuses to enter the house. His father comes out and pleads with him, but he remains adamant, insisting that he was always obedient and never was rewarded with even a small party, arguing that his wayward brother does not deserve this big banquet. The father replies tenderly that their father-son relationship endures and his two-thirds of the inheritance is still intact. Then stressing the ongoing relationship between his two sons, he insists: "But we had to celebrate and rejoice, because this brother of yours was dead and has come to life; he was lost and has been found" (Luke 15: 11-32).

The older son exemplifies important virtues, such as obedience, loyalty, hard work, and fidelity, which are worthy of praise as his father indicates. Yet he also represents a moralistic viewpoint that blinds him to the possibilities of repentance, forgiveness, and reconciliation. He interprets his brother's behavior as totally unacceptable, so grievous that it destroyed their sibling relationship. This not only precluded forgiveness but also fostered envy at his brother's good fortune and stifled any natural compassion he might feel for him. The father gets to the root of the problem by reminding his older son that relationships are prior to moral rules and are more important than bad behavior. It is, he insists, "Your brother who was lost and has been found."

We can find inspiration in Christians who live the truth of this Gospel. A single father, for example, maintains a loving relationship with his son despite the young man's many transgressions: lying, stealing, disrespect, drugs, and violence. He really does not like the rebellious teenager's behavior, but he continues to see him as his son. In order to maintain this relationship, the father prays regularly and relies on the support of friends. Following the advice of his pastor, he practices tough love and consistent discipline, which over time prove effective. Despite many setbacks, the wayward son eventually grows into a fine Christian adult, and the two now have a close and mutually enriching relationship.

> Can I identify with the older son in the Prodigal Son story?

35. Am I overly concerned with impressing others?

Luke tells us Jesus went to the house of a leading Pharisee and noticed that the guests were choosing the places of honor at table. In response, Jesus advised them not to take the highest place, because they might be embarrassed if the host asks them to move to make room for a more important guest. Rather, they should take the lowest place so they can enjoy the esteem of the other guests when the host invites them to move up to a higher position. Jesus then adds, "For all who exalt themselves will be humbled, and those who humble themselves will be exalted" (Luke 14: 7-14).

In applying this teaching to ourselves, we can be sure it is not a lesson in table etiquette nor is it advice on how to gain the esteem of others. It is a parable, as Luke informs us, that invites reflection on the importance of developing the virtue of humility in order to manage our need for public recognition.

We all know something of the need for affirmation, praise, respect, and recognition as well as the temptation to let this need get out of control: fishing for compliments, demanding constant affirmation, cutting corners to gain public recognition, and exaggerating to impress others.

Jesus proposes humility as the radical antidote to these temptations. Humble persons know and live the deepest truth of life: we are totally dependent on the God who loves us unconditionally. We are important and worthwhile only because God is our Father, Jesus is our Brother, and the Holy Spirit is our Advocate. Our essential task is to do the will of the Father, to participate in the mission of Christ, and to share the gift of the Spirit with others. We are not the center of the universe or the masters of our fate; but we all have talents and gifts that can contribute to the extension of the kingdom of God in the world.

When Christians develop the virtue of humility, they manage the need for affirmation more wisely and graciously. A wife who demanded constant expressions of love from her husband now rests more secure in the abiding love of God and her spouse. A junior executive who often worked extra stressful hours trying to impress his boss now puts in a good day's work, calmly confident he is doing his part to serve God and his company. A woman who constantly exaggerated to impress her friends now puts more effort into listening to them and understanding their needs. A man who regularly went to Mass to maintain the respect of family and friends now participates in the liturgy to praise God and to find nourishment for living the Christian life. In cases like these, humility tempers and guides the human desire for affirmation.

> What could I do to become a more humble person, more confident of my gifts and better able to manage my needs?

36. Do I tend to hold grudges?

"For where two or three are gathered in my name, I am there among them" (Matthew 18:20). This striking statement of Jesus, which has comforted his followers across the centuries, comes after he presented practical advice for reconciling disputes among his followers, starting with face-to-face, one-on-one encounters with offending persons. Jesus understood, better than any of the great prophets, the crucial importance of forgiveness and reconciliation in maintaining healthy relationships and viable communities. His presence in our communal lives is a great blessing, providing us with motivation and guidance as we strive to be reconcilers in our fragmented and polarized world. Empowered by the presence of Christ, our task is to repair broken relationships, to promote family harmony, to foster neighborhood cooperation, to encourage mutual respect within the parish community, to serve the common good of society, and to further the cause of world peace.

We can imagine individuals who have responded positively to the Gospel message and personally contributed to the great cause of reconciliation. A man long estranged from a former friend arranges lunch with him, where they talk out their differences and reestablish their friendship. A wife in the habit of waiting for her husband to apologize after a fight starts taking the initiative to reconcile, which enriches their marriage. A black woman seeks help from a white neighbor, and together they established an effective block-watch program that helps reduce crime in their neighborhood. A strong pro-life Catholic goes out of his way to meet a fellow parishioner committed to social justice, which leads to a friendship and mutual cooperation on a parish program to assist single mothers. A woman with a promising career in the pharmaceutical industry purposely befriends a social worker who encourages her to participate in a self-help program for the poor. A grandfather and longtime peace activist spends a lot of extra time with his college-educated, consumer-oriented grandson trying to get him to expand his interests, which eventually leads the boy to get involved in the peace-making efforts of Pax Christi.

In these examples, eyes of faith discern the presence of Christ who called us to be reconcilers and promised to be in our midst as we gather in his name and work to extend his kingdom.`

> How can I participate more effectively in Christ's mission of reconciliation?

37. Do I see myself as superior to others?

In Mark's Gospel, Jesus asks his disciples what they were arguing about as they travelled to Capernaum, but they remain silent. Mark tells us they were discussing who among them is the greatest. Jesus uses the opportunity to instruct the Twelve: "Whoever wants to be first must be last of all and servant of all" (Mark 9: 33-37).

We probably know something of the dynamics of the conversation that the disciples were reluctant to reveal. It has to do with the common human temptation to judge ourselves superior to others: deriving our self-worth from being better than someone else; and looking down on others as less worthy, talented or blessed.

Jesus suggests another way of living: less competitive and more cooperative; less effort to pull others down and more to lift them up; less emphasis on winning and more on doing our best. In the kingdom proclaimed by Christ, human beings do not strive to defeat others but to serve them, helping them develop their talents and reach their potential. Seeing ourselves not as masters but as servants puts us on a path of conversion that roots our self-worth in God's love for us as a unique individual.

We can imagine individuals who have found a way to appropriate this Gospel teaching. A small business owner finds things go better when he treats his employees as friends and colleagues. A woman feels better about herself when she avoids comparing herself to her more affluent friends. A teacher is more effective when he puts more emphasis on facilitating learning than maintaining discipline. A priest becomes a better pastor when he sets aside his authoritarian tendencies and dedicates himself to becoming a servant leader. A social worker finds more satisfaction in her job when she empathizes with clients as individuals sharing the common human journey. A woman religious gets along better with her superior when she sees her as a fellow human with strengths and weaknesses rather than just as an authority figure.

> In what specific way can I put into practice Christ's call to serve others?

38. Am I open to truth and goodness whenever it appears?

In Mark's Gospel, John the apostle says to Jesus: "Teacher, we saw someone casting out demons in your name, and we tried to stop him, because he was not following us." Jesus replies: "Do not stop him…. Whoever is not against us is for us" (Mark 9: 38-40).

In this passage, John represents religious exclusivism which can be expressed in various ways: we walk in the light, others journey in darkness; we are saved, others are lost; we are blessed with God's truth, others are cursed with Satan's lies; we lead moral lives, others are sinners; we are faithful Christians, others are Christian in name only. These extreme expressions of exclusivism invite reflection on more subtle forms that may lurk in our own souls.

Jesus, on the contrary, instructs us in a more open, inclusive religious outlook. He came to save all people. He reached out to those on the margins. He included in his inner circle individuals from various segments of society, including fishermen, a tax collector, and even a Zealot. His disciples eventually came to understand that Gentiles were included in the plan of salvation, that people of all nations can be saved, as can all who follow their conscience. People of various secular and religious backgrounds can contribute to spreading the reign of God. Christians can collaborate with all persons of good will to humanize culture and promote justice and peace. As Jesus put it, if they are not against us, they are for us!

We can hear witnesses responding personally to the inclusive message of Christ. "As a Catholic, I am learning more about my own faith as well as Islam from participating in a Christian Muslim Dialogue group." "In the past, I was afraid that my atheist father was going to be damned, but now I believe he is close to God because he is such a good man." "Since coming to college, I have gained great respect for my Jewish roommate who really lives the scriptural command to love our neighbor." "I am really glad that Pope Francis addressed his environment encyclical to all people of good will." "The Protestants on our Interfaith Peace and Justice Council are good at reminding us Catholics of the biblical warrant for our work." "Encouraged by a Hindu colleague, I started doing a Christian form of transcendental meditation each day." "The secular humanist in our Pax Christi group has helped us strengthen our anti-war position.

> How can I practice the inclusive teaching of Jesus?

39. Am I too controlling in my relationships?

Matthew tells the story of tenant farmers who were hired to tend a vineyard and go to extreme lengths to gain control of the vineyard for themselves, even to killing the owner's son (Matthew 21: 33-43). We can let the tenants represent the common human temptation to exercise excessive control over various aspects of our lives: for example, the dynamics of family life, the shape of friendships, the situation at work, and even the role of God. Sometimes the effort to gain or maintain control can hurt others as suggested by the murder of the owner's son. Parents constantly hovering over their teenage daughter have thwarted her emotional development. A wife, intent on getting her husband to be more like her father, has steadily eroded her spouse's confidence and increased his resentment. A sales manager, given to micromanaging his subordinates, has curtailed their creativity and, as a result, their productivity.

The parables of Jesus are designed to help us understand and live kingdom ideals. At the end of this Gospel passage, Jesus says the kingdom will be given to the people who produce its fruit. We could take this as a call to rise above the temptation to control others and enter into more fruitful relationships. Where God reigns, human beings relate to one another on the basis of equality and mutuality. In the kingdom of God, Christians, following the example of Jesus, set aside their own needs in order to help others grow and flourish.

We can detect the presence of the kingdom where relationships are not controlling but are empowering. Parents gradually educate their children into a life of responsible freedom so they can be healthy, interdependent adults. A pastor creates an atmosphere which encourages parishioners to take initiative in creating a vital faith community. The owner of a small company treats his employees like family, creating bonds of mutual respect and trust. A married couple improves their relationship by concentrating on helping each other grow spiritually. A social worker sees her clients not as a class of people who need help but as unique individuals called to take hold of their own lives. A second-grade teacher in a Catholic school thinks of her personal care for each student as an early contribution to their long journey to Christian adulthood. A member of a religious order tries to rise above her critical inclinations by identifying and encouraging the unique gifts of the sisters who live with her.

We can hear this Gospel passage as a challenge to our controlling tendencies and as an encouragement to develop more fruitful, empowering relationships.

> What is one practical step I could take to be less controlling and more empowering in my relationships?

40. What is my vision of an ideal marriage?

In the Gospel according to Mark, the Pharisees test Jesus by asking him if a husband can lawfully divorce his wife. Explaining that Moses permitted divorce because of "the hardness of your hearts," Jesus insists that husbands and wives "become one flesh," and "Therefore what God has joined together, let no one separate" (Mark 10: 2-16).

The scripture scholars tell us that Mark recorded this absolute prohibition of divorce around the year 70 A.D. and that Matthew, writing less than 20 years later, included an exception, permitting divorce for immorality. This suggests that we interpret the teaching of Jesus on marriage not as an absolute law but as representative of the high idealism found in the Gospels; for example, go the extra mile and turn the other cheek. Husband and wife becoming one flesh suggests an ideal never totally achieved but worthy of continued effort. Couples can never say they have a perfect marriage; they have totally achieved God's will for their union; they have done everything possible to help each other come closer to Christ. There is no place for self-righteousness or complacency in married life.

Christ does call couples to an ongoing effort to come closer to the Gospel ideal as exemplified in healthy marriages: a husband and wife work out separately a couple times a week to stay in better physical shape for each other; spouses arrange a date night once a month to have time to be attentive to one another; married partners read a book separately and find times to discuss it; newlyweds do a marriage encounter to improve their communication skills; a wife and husband have a difficult conversation on how they could do a better job of meeting each other's emotional needs; an elderly couple maintain their longstanding custom of discussing the Liturgy of the Word over brunch after Sunday Mass; a couple preparing for marriage both read the fourth chapter of *The Joy of Love*, the Apostolic Exhortation of Pope Francis, and spend a good deal of time discussing it together.

Reflection on the Gospel ideal of marriage reminds us that some couples cannot make it work despite good intentions and prudent efforts. Surely some marriages could be saved by good counselling, creative efforts, generous forgiveness, and deep prayer. Sometimes, however, divorce is necessary or the best of poor options. The Church officially recognizes this and should offer pastoral care: welcoming divorced persons to liturgy and communion; sponsoring support groups for them; offering counselling to wounded spouses; creating a climate of understanding aware of the difficulties of making marriage work in the contemporary world; and providing good marriage preparation programs.

> What does it mean to me personally to think of the teaching of Jesus on marriage as a high kingdom ideal?

41. Do I treat others as equals?

Mark informs us that the Zebedee brothers, James and John, were angling for high positions in the kingdom, much to the chagrin of the other ten. Jesus used the occasion to teach the Twelve that they should not lord it over others but should act as servants. He reminded them of his own mission: "For the Son of Man came not to be served but to serve" (Mark 10: 35-45). Furthermore, he lived out that vocation during his public ministry, exorcising demons, healing the sick, and preaching the good news.

This passage prompts reflection on ways we might be tempted to lord it over others: throwing our weight around; taking advantage of others; misusing our authority; exploiting the weakness of others; looking down on the less fortunate; putting on airs; portraying a sense of superiority; dominating conversations.

If we can detect in ourselves even quite subtle ways of dominating others, we are in a position to hear Christ calling us to act less like masters and more like servants, to be less self-centered and more attentive to ours.

We can imagine individuals who are trying to be more Christ-like in their relationships. A mother who interfered too much in her son's marriage now helps out only when asked. A husband who expected his wife to wait on him is now doing his share of the domestic chores. A father who generally ignored his daughter and her teenage activities now responds generously when she asks for his help. A very successful older brother who often fought with his younger sister now helps pay for her college education. A corporate executive who was overly harsh with one of her employees is now helping him to develop his skills so he can move up in the corporation. A pastor who thought of his flock as children needing fatherly guidance now sees himself as a servant leader, empowering his adult parishioners to use their gifts to build up the Body of Christ and spread the kingdom in the world. A municipal judge who tended to look down on the petty criminals before him became more compassionate, looking for ways to help rehabilitate them.

> How could I become a more faithful disciple of Christ, who came not to be served but to serve?

42. Am I guilty of stereotyping others?

In Mark's Gospel, Jesus returns to his hometown of Nazareth where he takes his turn teaching in the synagogue on the Sabbath. His fellow townsfolk, who knew him well and have heard of his mighty deeds, end up rejecting him, saying: "Is not this the carpenter, the son of Mary?" So Jesus, amazed at their lack of faith, was not able to perform any mighty deeds in his hometown, except curing a few sick people (Mark 6: 1-6).

It seems that the people of Nazareth had a restricted view of Jesus as a woodworker, which blinded them to his larger role as a prophet speaking for God: to them he was too ordinary to be doing such extraordinary deeds. They knew about his job and his relatives but were unable to appreciate his deeper inner reality as the Son of God. They were guilty of stereotyping Jesus, boxing him in, confining him to their preconceived notions.

We all know something of the temptation to view others in a stereotypical way, blinding us to their good qualities. Cultural stereotypes can influence our perceptions: people on welfare are lazy; corporate executives are hard hearted; politicians are corrupt; non-believers are selfish; Muslims are terrorists; Jews are God-killers; Evangelicals are uncritical fundamentalists. Such gross generalizations preclude nuanced perceptions of people as individuals who almost always exceed our limited judgements.

Jesus, himself the victim of stereotyping, was able to perceive the unique goodness in everyone he encountered. The Samaritan woman was not an enemy but a potential believing missionary. Zacchaeus was not just a chief tax collector but a man capable of reform and restitution. The example and teachings of Jesus encourage us to stay open to the often-surprising goodness and virtues of others.

We can imagine individuals who understand that message. A wife who for years thought of her hardworking, loving husband as spiritually tone deaf was delighted to discover that he actually had a rich spiritual life that he was reluctant to discuss. A Christian with a general mistrust of Muslims as violent people befriended a Muslim colleague at work and discovered a gentle, compassionate man. A woman with an intuitive dislike for her opinionated mother-in-law learned to avoid serious arguments with her and over time came to know her as a woman not only with strong opinions but also with a tender heart.

How can I do a better job of avoiding negative generalities and seeing the unique goodness of other people?

43. How can I act more like a Good Samaritan?

In Luke's Gospel, a lawyer tests Jesus by asking him what he should do to inherit eternal life (Luke 10: 25-37). Prompted by

Jesus, the lawyer answers the question himself by quoting two separate commandments in the Hebrew Scriptures: to love God with all your heart, soul, strength, and mind; and to love your neighbor as yourself. Jesus approves his answer, adding "do this and you will live."

To justify himself, the lawyer then asks Jesus: "And who is my neighbor?" Jesus answers by telling the Good Samaritan parable. A man going on the dangerous road from Jerusalem to Jericho falls victim to robbers and is left helpless on the side of the road. A priest and Levite see him but pass by, presumably to avoid ritual defilement. But a Samaritan, who is a despised half-breed by the Jews, is moved with compassion, stops, attends to the hurt man's wounds, gets him to an inn, and pays for his care. Jesus asks the lawyer which of the three "was neighbor" to the victim. The lawyer, somewhat reluctantly perhaps, responds "The one who showed him mercy." Jesus says, "Go and do likewise."

We notice that Jesus does not answer the question of who qualifies as a neighbor deserving of our love. The parable, rather, answers the question of who acts like a neighbor. The neighbor is one who extends mercy to someone in need. The good neighbor, like the Samaritan, is moved by compassion for those who are suffering. In a way, Jesus answered the first question about how to attain eternal life. We do gain life, here and hereafter, by loving others, by attending to those in need, by feeling compassion for those suffering, and by acting to make the situation better.

As our common language indicates, we admire the Good Samaritans in our midst. Some make the national news. In 1982, Lenny Skutnik, who worked for the U.S. Congressional Budget office, saw Air Florida Flight 90 crash into the freezing Potomac River. Only a few passengers survived the crash, but Skutnik saw a woman in the water, dove in, swam to her, and assisted her to the shore, saving her life. Less than a month later, President Reagan invited him to sit with the first lady at the State of the Union Address, where he received a long-standing ovation. The story reminds us that the teaching of Jesus on being a good neighbor remains a celebrated ideal in our world today.

Most Good Samaritan stories draw less attention: the black woman who does the shopping for her white neighbor while she was homebound; the motorist who stops to help a lady struggling to change a flat tire; the lawyer who does excellent pro bono work to keep a poor family from being unjustly evicted from their apartment. Such people generally remain anonymous but truly live the Gospel.

> Is there a particular person who needs my help right now?

44. How seriously do I take the Law of Love?

In John's Gospel, after informing his disciples that he will be leaving them soon Jesus declares: "Just as I have loved you, you also should love one another." He adds that this shared love among his disciples will be a sign to others that they are truly his followers (John 13: 33-35).

Love is central to the whole message of Jesus. God is love and shares divine love with all people of all times. Making an essential connection between two commands found in his Jewish heritage, Jesus taught us to love God wholeheartedly and to love our neighbor as ourselves. His command to love others includes those who are different from us, even our enemies.

Jesus not only taught the law of love, he practiced it in his own life. He ate with sinners, reached out to the marginalized, and forgave his persecutors. He gave himself completely to the cause of God and humanity, even to the point of dying on the cross for all human beings. He set his own life of self-giving love as the ideal to guide and encourage the efforts of his followers to love others as strongly as he had loved them.

John the evangelist puts the emphasis on love within the community of faith, among those who call themselves Christians. We find examples of this love wherever Christians gather, whether it is in small base communities or in large parishes. A very conservative Catholic went out of his way to befriend a progressive fellow parishioner, which led to periodic conversations over lunch where they have found some common ground and learned to respect each other's distinctive faith perspectives. The permanent members of a university parish provide free meals for collegians after the Sunday evening Mass. A middle-aged man who was unemployed for two years before finding a job started a support group for parishioners facing a similar predicament. A wealthy woman established scholarships for students to attend Catholic grade schools, high schools, and universities, enabling them to graduate free of debt. A Eucharistic Minister takes communion to the sick and spends extra time with each homebound person, befriending some and helping them in other ways. Simple acts of love like these within the community of faith do indeed make the Christian claim more credible, especially in our cynical world.

> What concrete act of love could I perform to fulfill Christ's command to love one another?

45. What can I learn from the Prodigal Son Parable about reconciliation?

Only the evangelist Luke tells us the marvelous Prodigal Son parable (Luke 15: 11-32). In response to the Pharisees and scribes who accuse him of eating with sinners, Jesus tells the story of a young man who defies convention by taking his share of his inheritance, going off to a distant country, squandering his money, and finding himself working for a Gentile tending swine, which was forbidden by Jewish law. He decides to return home to work for his father as a hired hand, but his father sees him coming, runs out to embrace him, and orders a sumptuous feast because "this son of mine was dead and is alive again; he was lost and is found!"

But there is more to the story. The elder son, who has always been faithful to his father, resents his father's celebration of his wayward son's return and refuses to attend the party. After telling his older son that "all that is mine is yours," the father tries to reestablish a brotherly relationship: "But we had to celebrate and rejoice, because this brother of yours was dead and has come to life; he was lost and has been found."

This classic story has a marvelous capacity to touch the hearts of those who reflect on it with an open mind and heart. A mother decides that she must be less judgmental and more forgiving in relating to her four children, each with their own distinct personality. A retired accountant, who has always thought of God as a divine bookkeeper, feels a sense of liberation when she thinks of God as even more forgiving than the father in the parable who does not demand an apology or an explanation but simply throws a party. A religious education director loves the analysis he read of the father's embrace: opening his arms to welcome his prodigal son; holding him close as a sign of loving forgiveness; and then opening his arms again to invite his prodigal son to find his own way to live out their restored relationship. A younger brother who has always been envious of his older brother recognizes that he has to be more tolerant and accepting of his sibling. A grandmother who has struggled to keep her family together finds herself rooting for the older son to go into the party because only this will avoid a permanent rupture in the family and make reconciliation possible.

> With which of the two sons do I most identify? Why?

46. Do I really try to love my enemies?

Luke tells us Jesus instructed his disciples, "Love your enemies, do good to those who hate you, bless those who curse you, pray for those who abuse you." This general injunction to love enemies applies to specific situations: for example, when someone strikes you on one cheek, offer him the other as well; when someone takes your coat, give him your shirt as well. Jesus then inserts a positive version of the Golden Rule: "Do to others as you would have them do to you." For his disciples, however, it is not enough to reciprocate the kindness offered by others. Rather, they are to love their enemies and do good to them; they are to lend without expecting anything back. Jesus presents his disciples with the highest ideal: "Be merciful, just as your Father is merciful." Those who strive for this ideal will be "children of the Most High" (Luke 6: 27-35).

This passage is taken from Luke's Great Sermon on the Plain, which shares common themes and similar language with Matthew's Sermon on the Mount, no doubt due to a presumed common source, called the Q document. The teaching of Jesus on love of enemies is an example of the high idealism found in the Gospels, which rules out self-righteous complacency and encourages persevering efforts to move toward the ideal.

Loving enemies defies logic and goes against common sense. The enemy might take forgiveness as a sign of weakness or a justification for another attack. But Jesus understood that only forgiving love can heal the wounds incurred when limited, fallible human beings interact. He insisted that the God of unconditional love calls us to participate in the great cause of reconciliation by praying for those who mistreat us and doing good to those who hate us.

Loving a person who has hurt us is often a challenging task that requires prayer and step-by-step perseverance, as this composite story suggests. Bill was happily married for over twenty years when suddenly his wife, Mary, announced she no longer wanted to be a wife or mother and left the family to do her own thing. At first, Bill was in shocked disbelief, but as all of his efforts at reconciliation were rebuffed, his shock hardened into angry resentment. After drifting along for a few months, he recommitted himself to caring for his two teenage children, vowing not to say anything negative about Mary. After the divorce was final, he encouraged his kids to reach out to their mother with emails and cards, even if they did not get a response. On the advice of his pastor, he began praying for Mary that she would find happiness and for himself that God would rid him of his lingering resentments. Over time, Bill's heart did soften and he felt the first glimmering of the grace of forgiveness. It was a little over five years after the divorce that he heard that Mary was in hospice care, suffering from a terminal brain tumor. Praying for wisdom, he went to visit her and they achieved a tearful reconciliation. During the next six months, Bill visited her periodically and was with her when she died. He was extremely pleased that their now adult children were also able to reconcile with their mother. The peace Bill felt at the funeral Mass stayed with him the rest of his life.

> Is there someone who has hurt me that I should forgive and what is my next step in that process?

47. Am I able to accept my limitations?

Luke tells us John, the son of Zachariah and Elizabeth, is out in the desert preaching good news and baptizing those who request it. He has created such a reputation that people are thinking he might be the Christ, the long-awaited Messiah, an expectation he could have fostered but instead vigorously denied, pointing instead to one who will baptize with the Holy Spirit and fire. Many people came to John asking advice, and he told them: "Whoever has two coats must share with anyone who has none." When despised tax collectors, who cooperated with the occupying Romans and often overcharged their fellow Jews, asked John what they should do, he replied: "Collect no more than the amount prescribed for you." John also admonished soldiers who protected the tax collectors not to practice extortion and to be satisfied with their wages (Luke 3: 10-18).

As we reflect on how to apply the Gospel to our lives today, we hear John the Baptist telling us to be generous to those in need, to accept our limitations, and to treat others justly. We can imagine individuals heeding this advice. Joyce has a lucrative job with an advertising firm that enables her to indulge her passion for fine clothes. For years she was in the habit of donating clothes she no longer needed or wanted to the annual Thanksgiving clothing drive. This year she made a prayerful decision to donate not only clothes she no long wanted but also some she liked and still wanted to wear. Having cleared out some space in her closet, she felt a new open space in her heart, which led to genuine prayers of gratitude. In that prayerful spirit, she resolved to look for other ways to share her material blessings with the less fortunate, not from her excess possessions but from her heart.

Greg, a middle-age business man, has always been envious of his older brother who was a better athlete in high school and became far more successful in the business world. Desperate to outdo his brother, Greg started his own business, made some shady deals, treated his few employees badly, lost money, and had to shut down. Hitting bottom, Greg was forced into an intense period of reflection that revealed to him his sin of envy, which had led to his destructive behavior. He came to see a path forward: repentance for his sins against others; learning to accept himself with his strengths and weaknesses; coming to terms with his limitations; and replacing his envy of his brother with fraternal love.

48. How can I improve my friendships?

John the evangelist assures us that Christ does not call us slaves but calls us friends (John 15: 9-17). He shares with us the secrets of his heavenly Father, who loves us unconditionally. He encourages us to use his name in putting our petitions before God.

So, our friendship with Christ should be the source of a deep and abiding joy, but it also places fundamental demands on us. We are to remain in his love by keeping his commandments. He calls us to love one another as he has loved us. Our Christian vocation is to share his self-sacrificing love for us with others and to do so with a joyful spirit.

The Gospel invites reflection on our own friendships. We do not choose our parents or siblings, but we do choose our friends. We like to spend time with them and to do things together. If we are blessed with good friends, prayers of gratitude are certainly in order. A husband who considers his wife his best friend thanks God every day for this blessing.

Loyalty is a crucial virtue for maintaining friendships. We think of Mary of Magdala, who remained faithful to Jesus through his passion and death. Donna, a collegian, stood by her pregnant friend after she was abandoned by the father and was there for the woman through the birth and beyond.

Friendships can go badly, of course: misunderstandings, disappointments, inattention, and even betrayal. This makes forgiveness essential to maintaining and restoring friendships. We learn from Christ who forgave his friends even as they abandoned him, later offering them a greeting of peace and an opportunity to start over with him. Following the example of the Lord, a small business owner not only forgave his friend who stole some money from the company but managed to restore their friendship over a period of time.

> What can I learn from Christ about deepening and strengthening my friendships?

49. Am I satisfied with my community involvement?

The evangelist Mark tells the story of a leper who comes to Jesus seeking healing. Moved with pity, Jesus touches him and says: "Be made clean!" After curing the man, Jesus warns him sternly not to tell anyone and advises him to show himself to the priest (Mark 1: 40-45).

The detail about seeing the priest is extremely important, because it reveals Jesus not only as a healer but also as a community builder. Lepers in that society were total outcasts, banished to the margins, forbidden contact with their families and the community gathered for prayer. Only the priest could authenticate the cleansing so that the healed leper could return to his family and synagogue services.

Making sure the leper is reunited with loved ones is typical of Jesus, who put such emphasis on forming community. To fulfill his mission to restore Israel to covenant fidelity, Jesus chose the Twelve, representing the twelve tribes of Israel, and worked to form them (albeit with limited initial success) into a community of faithful disciples. He taught them to love one another and insisted on forgiveness as the antidote to community breakdowns. By instructing his disciples to address God as "Abba" or "Father" in prayer, he created a permanent reminder that we are all members of God's family, brothers and sisters to one another in a beloved community.

By virtue of our baptism, we share in the community forming mission of Christ. Parents participate by creating families where the bonds of love are stronger than individual differences and interests. Neighbors contribute by extending a helping hand to those in need. Citizens help by working with others for the common good. Workers do their part by striving to humanize the worksite. Parishioners share in the mission by using their gifts to make parishes more credible signs and instruments of the kingdom. Members of religious communities offer explicit witness to the communal dimension of Christ's ministry. All Christians share in the community building mission of Christ by overcoming selfishness and practicing the law of love in the various communal settings that constitute our lives as social creatures.

> Do I appreciate the community-forming mission of Christ and how I could become a more constructive contributor?

50. How do I relate to my deceased loved ones?

We may find ourselves periodically reflecting on our deceased loved ones, who no longer walk this earth with us, leaving an empty space in our hearts. The Bread of Life discourse in the Gospel of John, offers us hope that our departed loved ones are in the hands of God, now permanent members of the Communion of Saints (John 6: 22-50). Highlighting his Father's will that everyone who believes in the Son will have eternal life, Jesus assures the crowds: "Anyone who comes to me I will never drive away." These words offer comfort to us who ponder the ultimate fate of our deceased loved ones. As does this passage in Wisdom: "But the souls of the righteous are in the hand of God, and no torment will ever touch them (Wisdom 3: 1). Our Christian faith assures us that Christ, who was raised to life by his Father, has conquered death, so that we who have died with him in baptism may live with him in newness of life. The Second Vatican Council supported and extended this salvation optimism by teaching that God does not deny the grace of salvation—even to those who have not yet learned to call him by name but do follow their conscience (The Light of the Nations, 16).

Hope in God's saving mercy can free us for fruitful reflection on those who are now in the hands of God. A widow of two years who endured a long marriage with a controlling husband asks God for the grace to rise above the resentment that still hardens her heart. A collegian who worried about the salvation of his atheist grandfather finds contentment in the hope that God has rewarded him for living a virtuous life in accord with his conscience. A mother who helplessly watched her troubled son gradually kill himself with drugs finds comfort in the belief that he now shares a totally new life with Christ. A successful executive who often took her blessings for granted now thanks God for her deceased parents who made many sacrifices so she could get a first class education. A young married man who tended to put work before his family, dedicates himself to following the good example of his father, who always put family first.

We do well to reflect on our deceased loved ones, now with God forever, grateful for their ongoing support, ready to heal any lingering wounds, and committed to emulating their virtues.

> How can I best honor the deceased who touched my life most profoundly?

Chapter Three

The Doctrine of God
(reflecting on the Gracious Mystery)

51. Am I too busy to pray and rest?

Mark tells us that the apostles, having returned from an apparently successful and exhausting missionary journey, report to Jesus all they had done and taught. His response is: "Come away to a deserted place all by yourselves and rest a while." As the story goes on, the apostles have trouble following the wise advice of the Master because people were coming to them in great numbers and a vast crowd greeted them when they arrived at their getaway (Mark 6: 30-34).

Christ's advice to get away and rest seems especially important to those of us who are caught up in the busyness and demands of everyday life. We can interpret Christ's advice in various ways: to provide for more leisure time in the midst of heavy demands; to carve out time for prayer and meditation in our daily schedule; to get proper exercise each day; to enjoy vacations that are truly relaxing and not an extension of work.

We all know people who have found ways to follow Christ's advice despite hectic schedules. A mother who also works outside the home gets up ten minutes early and spends the time in prayer and reflection. A busy executive stops in his parish church on his way home from work for a few minutes of recollection and prayer. A married couple arranges a date night periodically to just enjoy each other's company. A single woman with a demanding job gets to the gym for vigorous exercise at least twice a week. A family takes a simple vacation near their home that allows them to gear down and renew their spirits. A busy pastor, responsible for two parishes, uses his time driving between them to reflect on his ministry and to pray for the people he serves.

> What does Christ's advice to get away and rest mean to me personally and how could I follow it more effectively and creatively?

52. How can I find joy in life?

In the fourth Gospel, John the Baptist identified himself as "the voice of one crying out in the wilderness, 'Make straight the way of the Lord,'" (John 1: 19-28). He made it clear he was not Elijah or the Christ. Despite drawing large crowds, he stepped off center stage and directed the spotlight to Jesus. In the popular imagination, the Baptist is a stern prophet, a disciplined ascetic, a strict teacher. Perhaps we could also see him as a Spirit-filled man who maintained a joyful spirit despite facing grave hardships and threats.

In contrast to happiness, which is dependent on circumstances matching our desires, joy is a deep abiding sense of wellbeing, an inner peace that can survive bad things happening. In our Christian tradition, joy is a fruit of the Holy Spirit, a free gift from God, a byproduct of putting on the mind of Christ. We cannot buy joy; when it is directly sought, joy eludes us.

Some joyful people seem to be especially attentive to the Spirit abiding in them. It grounds them in a rich prayer life. Their disciplined lifestyle enables them to respond to the moral demands of the Advocate, one of Jesus' names for the Spirit. Their practice of reflective silence attunes them to the voice of the Spirit. In the book of Isaiah, the Servant of the Lord who attends to the poor, the broken hearted, and the captives, can say: "I will greatly rejoice in the LORD, my whole being shall exult in my God" suggesting to us that joy is connected with a life of service to those in need (Isaiah 61: 10-11). Although we cannot *earn* the gift of joy, we can *prepare ourselves for it* by daily prayer, healthy discipline, reflective meditation, and dedicated service.

Gloria, a single white woman, teaches first grade in an inner city, mostly black Catholic school. She loves her students, gives them extra time and attention, and prays for them every day. Despite limited finances and a restricted social life, Gloria is a joyful person, grateful to God for the gift of inner peace, which feels to her like a gentle stream running quietly through the depths of her soul.

Mike, a happily married man with two healthy children and a fulfilling job, was diagnosed with Parkinson's disease, sending him into an unhappy state of confusion and anxiety. He sought help from a counselor, but he remained depressed over his situation. One Sunday at Mass, when he received Christ in communion, Mike experienced a deep sense of joy, which felt like a lava flow from a volcanic eruption that spread and solidified throughout his whole being. It was a new sensation for him, unlike the happiness he had frequently enjoyed before in his life. This joy made him feel more dependent on God, closer to his family, and better able to cope with his illness, all of which produced in him a deeper sense of gratitude than he had ever known before.

> What are my own experiences of joy and do they lead me to prayers of gratitude?

53. Is my relationship to God influenced by marketplace values?

John's portrayal of the Cleansing of the Temple occurs early in the ministry of Jesus, when he goes up to Jerusalem to celebrate the Feast of Passover. Entering the Temple area, he makes a whip out of cords and drives out the sellers of sacrificial animals and the money changers, saying "stop making my Father's house into a market place" (John 2: 13-16).

It is not immediately clear why Jesus was so angry. Jews coming from all over to celebrate Passover needed to exchange their Roman coins in order to buy the animals for sacrifice. Biblical scholars suggest Jesus was fulfilling a prophecy of Zechariah that at the end-time there would be no need for merchants in the Temple. Through his symbolic action, Jesus was claiming that the new age had arrived and that he himself was replacing the Temple as the primary place where God and humans meet.

Perhaps we could extend this scholarly analysis and see the symbolic action of Jesus as a general challenge to the commodification of religion, which interprets the divine-human relationship in economic terms and marketplace values. We see this in the popular idea that we can earn heaven through meritorious actions, as well as in the notion that we can make deals with God, gaining earthly blessings in return for prayer and ascetical practices. The Gospel of prosperity, which promises worldly success to committed Christians, distorts the teaching of Jesus and reinforces a consumerist outlook. A marketplace mentality can move pastoral ministers to favor the big contributors and incline affluent parishioners to look down on the poor as lazy or less committed.

By proclaiming himself as the new center of our connection with God, replacing the Temple, Jesus invites a radical rethinking of the divine-human relationship based not on economics but on love. We cannot manipulate God through deals, bargains, even prayers or religious practices. We don't have to ask or even wait for God's love; it is always there. We just need to do our part.

We can imagine individuals who appropriate this slant on the Gospel. A collegian decides to study hard for final exams rather than relying on a last-minute novena for success. A pastoral leader purposely avoids knowing what parishioners contribute to the parish so she is not tempted to favor the big donors. A successful businessperson tries to overcome his stereotypical view of the poor as lazy by helping out a family living below the poverty line even though both the father and the mother are employed. An elderly Catholic who has always imagined God as a divine bookkeeper keeping track of our sins and good deeds, consciously strives to see God more like her own mother, who generously sacrificed everything to care for her children.

> What could I do to purify my relationship with God?

54. What is the relationship between my Image of God and my self-image?

As the great spiritual masters have recognized, there is a close connection between our image of God and the way we understand ourselves and our world. Negative perceptions of God correlate with dysfunctional self-images. For example, harsh images of God can contribute to low self-esteem. A narrow exclusive sense of God's providence can ground bias and prejudice. An emphasis on divine wrath can produce an unhealthy fear of damnation.

John's Gospel emphasizes God's love for us and our world manifested in sending Christ as our Savior (John 3: 16) and the Spirit as our Advocate (John 14: 26). Jesus, the Word made flesh, reveals a God not of wrath, but of overflowing love, a God who does not condemn the world but wills to save it. The God of love gives us the gift of eternal life, a gift that we already share as we make our journey in this world. As Christians, we name this gift the Holy Spirit, who lives within us as the source of our personal worth and community life. It was only later in the fourth century that the Church, building on the New Testament notion of the two related missions of the Word and of the Spirit, formulated the Trinitarian doctrine that the one God exists as three Persons. The Triune God, a communion of love, invites us to share in the overflowing divine life, thereby solidly grounding a positive understanding of ourselves and our relationships.

A story to illustrate the connection between God image and self-understanding. Eve grew up in a Catholic family with a harsh judgmental father and a loving mother, who gracefully endured serious health problems. Her image of God, largely derived from her father, of a demanding Father in heaven, left her with low self-esteem and a fear of damnation. Early in her marriage to a Catholic with a similar background, she and her husband made a charismatic retreat together, which emphasized the great gifts of the Holy Spirit they each received. For Eve, the retreat was life-changing. She developed a very positive image of God as a loving Source of good gifts which enabled her to gain greater self-confidence and better manage her fears. For over 20 years she lived a Spirit-filled life, positive about herself, her marriage, her Catholic faith, and her God. Then one day, her husband unexpectedly left her, without any adequate explanation, and her whole world collapsed. Eve could not pray, stopped going to Mass, hated her husband, and felt betrayed by God. Her positive image of God did not encompass tragedy. As part of her therapy, she consulted with a spiritual director who helped her develop a new maternal image of God, reflecting her mother's acceptance of suffering, a loving God who not only sent the Holy Spirit as the Source of good gifts, but also sent the Son to save, heal and liberate us by his cross and resurrection. Strengthened and guided by her maternal image of God, Eve was able to resume regular prayer and worship and to develop a renewed confidence that she could indeed manage the heavy cross imposed on her.

John's Gospel helps us develop a positive image of God so that we can live with greater confidence and effectiveness.

> What is my own dominate image of God and how does it influence my life?

55. What can I learn by reflecting on the Trinity?

In Matthew's Gospel, after the death of Jesus, eleven disciples assembled on a mountain in Galilee, as the Master had ordered them. Appearing to them, the risen Lord commissioned them to make disciples of all nations, baptizing them in the name of the Father, and of the Son and of the Holy Spirit, and teaching them to observe all that he had commanded them (Matthew 28: 16-20).

As Christians we were initiated into the community of faith by that very same Trinitarian formula. Through baptism, we are embraced by the Father's love, called to share in Christ's death and resurrection, and empowered by the Holy Spirit to spread the kingdom in the world. We are Trinitarian Monotheists, believers in one God who is personally present to us in three ways: as our Creator we call the one God our Father; as a participant in our history, we call the one God the Word, Son, or Logos; and as the continuing Source of our gifted existence we call the one God the Holy Spirit or our Advocate.

The doctrine of the Trinity, foreshadowed in today's Gospel, and more fully developed in the fourth century, serves as a reminder that our God is ultimately mysterious, beyond all imagining, greater than our power of reason, an inexhaustible source of love. As Thomas Aquinas insisted, the most important thing to know about God is that we cannot fully comprehend God. At the same time, our experience of the triune God active in our lives, tells us something true about the trinitarian character of the One God.

We can imagine various individuals enlightened by prayerful reflection on the Trinity offering personal testimony on how it enriches their Christian life. Because of my own reflection on the Trinity, I am now: more confident in dialogue with my Muslim friends about belief in one God; more conscious of how limited is my own understanding of God; more open to hearing others talk about their image of God; more attentive to the role of the Holy Spirit in my life; more committed to my baptismal vows; more dedicated to the mission of Christ; more aware of God's loving presence in my life; more attuned to the trinitarian form of liturgical prayer, which praises the Father through the Son in the unity of the Holy Spirit.

Which of these examples seems most significant to me?

56. How can I take better advantage of life's opportunities?

Matthew compares the kingdom of heaven to a king who prepares a sumptuous banquet to celebrate his son's wedding (Matthew 22: 1-14). When the invited guests refuse to come, the king sends his servants to invite everyone they find on the streets, filling the banquet hall with guests. Jesus uses the scriptural image of a lavish banquet to suggest the ultimate triumph of God's abundant grace, much as the prophet Isaiah spoke of a joyous day when God will provide for all peoples a feast of rich food and choice wines. For Jesus, this great feast represents not only a final victory of divine grace, but also a present reality filled with opportunities for spiritual growth. God's healing, reconciling, and liberating grace is available now. The reign is already here in our midst.

Open to all, the kingdom is filled with resources for personal growth, deeper relationships, and societal transformation. It is possible, however, as the parable suggests, to refuse the invitation to the feast, to miss the opportunities to cooperate with God's grace, to ignore the immense resources available in the kingdom.

A woman who was forced by circumstances to divorce her insensitive, self-centered husband, speaks truly when she says he missed a great opportunity to get to know a good person who loved him. A retired accountant still passes up all the adult religious education opportunities provided by his parish on the assumption that his grade school understanding of the faith is good enough for him. A woman who quit school to get married at a young age and has raised four children wants to go back to finish her college education but can't summon the courage to give it a try. An attorney has maintained his habit of attending Sunday Mass but has done little to make it a more fruitful experience. These examples of missed opportunities can prompt reflection on ways we often fail to tap the spiritual resources so abundantly available in the kingdom.

The parable of the banquet also suggests the good news that God is a gracious host who wants everyone to share in the blessings of the kingdom. Our God wants all people to be saved and participate in the feast of grace already present in our daily experience. Where God reigns, there are always new opportunities for spiritual growth. Spouses can help each other come closer to Christ by praying together. Individuals can find deeper meaning in their daily work by viewing it as their contribution to the spread of the kingdom in the world. American students can gain more from their collegiate experience by befriending international students. Worshipers can get more out of the Sunday liturgy by reflecting on the scripture readings ahead of time. Parishioners can gain a deeper understanding of their faith by attending parish-sponsored religious education programs for adults.

> How could I take better advantage of the lavish banquet prepared by the Gracious Host for all people?

57. How can I overcome anxiety and multiply my talents?

In the Gospel parable in Matthew, the master goes on a long journey, leaving his servants in charge of large sums of money: one five talents, another two talents and a third one talent, each according to his ability. After a long time, the master returns to settle accounts with his servants. The first two, who doubled their talents, receive high praise. Oddly, the master severely chastises the third servant for burying his money in the ground, presumably because his fears kept him from being productive. (Matthew 25:14-30).

With this interpretation, the parable suggests that we should not allow fears or excessive caution to dominate our lives. Fear can darken our consciousness, weaken our will and impede our activities. It can move us to bury our talents, bypassing opportunities for personal growth, healthy relationships, and community service.

More positively, the parable calls us to multiply our talents so we can participate more effectively in the mission of Christ. Jesus teaches us, by example and word, to trust God, enabling us to be less fearful and more creative. Christ sends us the Holy Spirit as our guide and strength so we can rise above our fears and act boldly and courageously on behalf of the kingdom. Liberated from paralyzing fears, believers have the opportunity to serve the common good by a life of discipleship that is productive and joyful.

We can think of contemporary examples of putting this Gospel message into practice. A wife, long dissatisfied with her sexual relationship with her husband, finally gets the courage to tell him what would help her enjoy sex more and is extremely pleased that she did so. A very affluent couple, married for almost forty years, overcome their irrational fear of running out of money and double their charitable giving from one to two percent of their annual income. A young man overcomes his fear of rejection and asks his dream girl for a date, and after ten years of a happy marriage still thanks God for that moment of grace. A gay man in his twenties eventually gets the courage to tell his family about his sexual orientation and now enjoys full acceptance by his parents and siblings. A single woman, who finds out she was getting paid less than her male colleagues, takes the risk of complaining to her boss and receives a substantial raise.

Not every fear is irrational or paralyzing. Not every exercise of the virtue of fortitude is effective or productive. Most of us, however, can recall times when the gift of courage overcame our fears and good things happened. Such experiences deserve prayers of gratitude and prepare us for the next time we are tempted to bury our talents out of fear.

> Can I recall a specific instance when I, by the grace of God, overcame my fear, allowing some blessing to flow?

58. How can I best prepare for the future?

In Mark's Gospel, Jesus speaks to his disciples about the end of time, the last days: the sun will be darkened and the stars will fall from the sky; the Son of Man will come on the clouds, with great power to gather his elect; stay alert to the signs that the end is coming; of that day or hour no one knows, not the angels, not the Son, but only the Father (Mark 13: 32).

The scripture scholars tell us that this passage reflects the "apocalyptic outlook," prevalent in the Jewish world at the time of Jesus, which expected God to intervene quickly and decisively in history to save his people suffering under Roman rule. How are we to interpret this passage today, when most people are not expecting an imminent end of the world? Perhaps we can see it as encouraging us to develop a healthy attitude toward the future which remains essentially unknowable.

For some people, the essential problem is excessive worry and anxiety over a future which appears dark, dangerous, and scary. To those who know something of this tendency, the Gospel speaks comforting words: remain calm despite all the chaos, because the Son of Man, Christ himself, will come to gather his people; the God who alone knows the future is totally trustworthy and will not abandon us; the frightening future is under the guidance of the Holy Spirit, the source of a light more powerful than all the dark forces.

We can imagine people appropriating this message in various ways. Facing an important job interview, a very anxious recent college graduate manages to stay calm enough to do well in the interview. A middle-aged woman finds the strength to make it through a dreaded regimen of chemotherapy treatment for breast cancer. A senior citizen terribly anxious about dying becomes peaceful in the last month before his death.

Others are not concerned enough about the future: drifting through life; putting things off; expecting things to get better without proper effort; falling into complacency; ignoring signs of impending trouble; making poor decisions without considering the future consequences. To those who experience this temptation, the Gospel has a sharp message: be prepared for the unexpected; actions have consequences; we have a limited number of tomorrows; one day we all stand before the merciful and just Judge.

We can also envision people who got this message. An engaged couple decides that saving intercourse for marriage would help them develop other ways of communicating and relating. A husband, who for years missed the April tax deadline, causing serious distress to his wife, starts filing early, leaving him with a much happier spouse. A single man who never worried about the future takes out an insurance policy to cover nursing home expenses so he would not be a burden on his younger sister if he is incapacitated.

59. How can I better manage my fears?

Matthew tells us Jesus encouraged the Twelve to fear no one (Matthew 10: 26-33). As disciples, their task is to proclaim the truth revealed by their Master. They are to acknowledge Jesus before others. As they participate in Christ's mission, they will face not only physical dangers but also spiritual attacks, which are even more frightening. Nevertheless, they are not to be afraid because the omnipotent God, who knows when a sparrow falls to the ground, cares for them as human beings worth more than many sparrows. Furthermore, Jesus will acknowledge his faithful disciples before his heavenly Father, a promise made to alleviate their fears.

As human beings we all know something of fear. We are not in total control of our lives nor are we completely integrated and totally mature persons. Our world is a mix of grace and sin, meaning we cannot avoid confrontations with dangerous evil forces. Some fears are helpful, others harmful; some are reasonable, others defy logic; some are superficial, others are deeper and are properly named anxieties; some are part of common human existence, others result from fidelity to our Christian vocation. In dealing with fear, the Gospel teaches us to trust God, who loves us as unique individuals, and to have confidence in Christ, who intercedes for us. Faith does not eliminate all our fears, but it does help us understand and manage them. A faith perspective helps in various ways: to use fears to promote personal growth; to unmask irrational fears; to name anxieties; to cultivate the virtue of fortitude; and to pray for strength.

We can find inspiration in individuals who have managed their fears in constructive ways. A nurse uses her fear of lung cancer to stop smoking. A junior executive who is afraid to speak up in meetings takes a seminar on public speaking and overcomes his fear. A father who is afraid to fly endures a flight to attend his daughter's graduation by meditating on the Gospel story of Jesus calming the storm. An elderly woman who was terribly anxious about death and judgment learns to trust God and dies peacefully. A deacon who fears recrimination for preaching on social justice in his all-white parish summons the courage to preach a prophetic homily and bears the ensuing criticism with surprising grace.

> What is my most troubling fear and how could my faith help me overcome it?

60. How can I become a more trusting person?

In Luke's Gospel someone asks Jesus: "Lord, will only a few be saved?" Avoiding a direct answer to the question, Jesus replies: "Strive to enter through the narrow door." He goes on to suggest to his Jewish audience that some self-righteous people may find themselves excluded from the kingdom while Gentiles from all over the world will participate in the heavenly banquet (Luke 13: 22-30).

Many Christians today hear this passage with a generally optimistic attitude on salvation. The Second Vatican Council taught that God's grace of salvation is available for all people, even atheists, provided they follow their conscience. Fewer Christians today worry about being damned to hell and more believe in a loving merciful God. Given this situation, the Gospel injunction to enter by the narrow gate functions as a warning against complacency: taking the gift of salvation for granted, taking the easy way out, neglecting prayer, avoiding discipline. Trusting in God's mercy does not give us the right to test God. Salvation optimism does not negate taking up the cross or make the Christian life easy. On the contrary, it should move us to be more generous, dedicated, disciplined, and prayerful followers of Christ. Freed from excessive guilt and confident in God's mercy, some Christians have made great progress in the spiritual life and become more effective disciples.

A woman who suffers from scrupulosity and routinely mentions questionable sins in her monthly confession gradually comes to appreciate the saving power of God's grace, which frees her from excessive guilt feelings. She now celebrates the Sacrament of Reconciliation more effectively, confessing just one of her sins and accepting a penance that will help her overcome it. A nurse who has great difficulty controlling his emotions when caring for dying patients comes to see death as a passageway to a more fulfilling life with God. He now does a better job of listening to his terminal patients and attending to their physical and spiritual needs.

> What could I do to deepen my trust in God's mercy?

61. What are my top priorities?

In Luke's Gospel Jesus informs a great crowd: "Whoever comes to me and does not hate father and mother, wife and children, brothers and sisters, yes, and even life itself, cannot be my disciple" (Luke 14: 25-26).

Given the great emphasis Jesus put on loving our neighbor and even our enemies, we cannot take this passage literally. The Aramaic language and the Near Eastern culture shared by Jesus tended to make comparisons by means of sharp contrasts. In the Hebrew scriptures, for instance, God says he hates ritual sacrifices but wants obedience, which we interpret not as a total repudiation of ritual worship but as a reminder that living a life of fidelity to God is more important. In a similar way, we can interpret the Gospel as teaching us that following Christ is even more important than the fundamental obligation of attending to our family members. Our most important relationship is to God. Our highest calling is to participate in the mission of Christ. Spreading the kingdom deserves our best efforts. Living these Gospel priorities actually helps us develop more loving personal relationships, including within our family circle as the following examples indicate.

A husband and wife both work extra hours so they can give their two children every possible material thing they want. At some point, however, they both come to realize that their children are out-of-control, spoiled, materialistic gluttons with insatiable desires for more and more things. Dismayed, the parents reflect on the Gospel, which leads to a conscious decision to get more serious about practicing their Catholic faith, simplifying their own lifestyle, and committing themselves to the arduous task of redirecting their teenage children. Realizing that family history and cultural trends are against them, they turn to God, asking forgiveness for their misguided childrearing and for strength to remain faithful to their new spiritual lifestyle, hoping that over time their good example will have a positive impact on their children. Their initial efforts will most likely encounter great opposition, intensified by a large dose of teenage rebellion. Over the long haul, however, frequent conversations, consistent discipline, and shared prayer will make a difference in gradually reorienting their children's priorities to reflect Gospel values. Someday the family will be able to laugh about the past and rejoice in their shared Christian journey with gratitude to God.

> What could I do to get my priorities more in line with the Christian value system?

62. Am I in danger of putting God to the test?

In his temptation account, Matthew contrasts Jesus, who fasts for 40 days and 40 nights in preparation for his victorious confrontation with the devil, with ancient Israel that periodically succumbed to temptations during its 40 years in the wilderness. Each of the three temptations, (to turn stones into bread, to jump down from the pinnacle of the Temple and to worship Satan), represents common human struggles against dark forces that we all can recognize. (Matthew 4: 1-11).

The second one, for example, where Satan takes Jesus to the top of the Temple in Jerusalem and tells him to jump down without getting hurt, suggests some common temptations: to take risks expecting divine help; to act dangerously without considering the consequences; and to rely on the spectacular at the expense of daily effort. As in the other temptations, Jesus responds decisively, trusting in God and drawing on his religious heritage by quoting the book of Deuteronomy: "Worship the Lord your God and serve only him."

Jesus is not going to use a spectacular gimmick to promote his cause but instead intends to persevere in the daily task of preaching the good news and establishing the reign of God. He will not tempt God, but will follow the will of his Father, obedient even to death on a cross. Satan may be clever and relentless, but Jesus will remain faithful to God and committed to his mission.

The Gospel reminds us that temptations are built into human existence. Jesus, the best of us, could not avoid them, nor can we. We can follow his example by trusting God, relying on our Christian faith, and acting decisively: a man is inclined to drive himself home after drinking heavily at a party, but listens to a friend and accepts a ride; a woman who has for years endangered her health by smoking decides she owes it to her family to kick the habit; a collegian invited to experiment with cocaine declines because he fears addiction; a middle aged woman who has ignored her weight problem for years, decides to follow better eating patterns and to exercise regularly; spouses who have tolerated a troubled marriage for years decide, for the sake of their kids, to get professional help; a social worker, who interacts daily with the poor, revives his long neglected daily prayer routine so as not to lose his sense of compassion and become jaded; a woman suffering from severe depression and suicidal thoughts reflects on the Scriptures and decides to get back on her medication lest she tempt God.

Reflection on the temptations of Christ becomes more fruitful when we identify specific ways that we are tempted to test God, and then commit ourselves to concrete remedial action based on the example of Jesus.

> Can I identify a specific way I am tempted to test God and how can I overcome this temptation?

63. Am I bothered by guilt feelings?

John's Gospel sets the scene: it is Sunday evening, the third day after the death of Jesus, and his disciples have locked themselves in for fear of the religious authorities (John 20:19-23). These are the disciples who in various ways were disloyal to their Master: Peter, James, and John fell asleep when Jesus asks them to pray; they all flee when Jesus is arrested; Peter denies knowing Jesus when challenged by a maidservant. We can imagine the disciples gathered in that locked room, burdened by a profound sense of guilt and paralyzed by self-loathing.

Then Jesus, the Innocent Victim, the Master Betrayed, the risen Christ, appears in their midst. We might expect some harsh words, or a mild rebuke, or a homily on loyalty. But what we do hear is, "Peace be with you": healing, reconciling, forgiving words. Jesus breaks the usual pattern of recrimination by substituting forgiveness for vengeance and reconciliation for accusation. Freed from guilt and self-loathing by divine mercy, the disciples rejoice.

The good news is that God's mercy, mediated by Christ, is always available to us. We are not imprisoned in our faults nor defined by our sins. Most of us have some experiential knowledge of divine mercy received or shared. A man with a serious gambling problem hits bottom and loses his house, but he gets a second chance and makes the most of it. A woman who for years confesses to being judgmental without ever seeing any progress in her behavior, arrives at Easter one year with a more open and tolerant attitude toward others. A father who has ostracized his son for being gay comes to full acceptance of his son, which is followed by a tearful reconciliation. A successful doctor who for years has put his career above his family realizes his misplaced priorities, asks forgiveness from his wife and children, and together they establish closer relationships. A traditional Catholic who confesses racial prejudice to a priest is inspired to serve as a Big Sister to a young black girl.

> How have I experienced God's mercy in my own life?

64. What role does the Holy Spirit play in my life?

In his farewell discourse at the Last Supper, Jesus tells his disciples they should be happy that he is leaving them and going to the Father because they, in turn, will receive the Advocate, sent by the Father, who will teach them "everything" and remind them of all Jesus has told them. Jesus will no longer walk with his disciples, but they will have the Holy Spirit living within them who will guide and strengthen them as they carry on the mission of Christ in the world (John 14: 23-29). The Holy Spirit is called the "Advocate or Paraclete," who testifies, like a legal witness, on behalf of Jesus and enables his disciples to testify to the life and teaching of their Master. The Advocate is "the Spirit of truth" who helps the disciples understand the deeper meaning of the teachings of Jesus.

Our Christian belief is that the Holy Spirit, sent by the Father in the name of Jesus, remains with us today, functioning as our companion, teacher, advocate, and judge. Historically, the Eastern Church has maintained a livelier sense of the role of the Holy Spirit than we have in the West. Pope John Paul II encouraged us "to breathe out of both lungs," the Eastern and Western branches of Christianity, suggesting that we incorporate a more vigorous theology of the Holy Spirit into our Western spirituality that has put more emphasis on the Father and the Son.

Due to a number of factors, Christians today are more likely to give testimony to the activity of the Holy Spirit in their lives. A mother says: "I felt the Spirit nudging me to be more attentive to the needs of my youngest son." A divorced man testifies: "It was only by the power of the Holy Spirit that I was able to forgive my ex-wife." A daughter confesses: "After many years I finally got up the courage to challenge the sexist attitudes of my father, for which I am very grateful to the Spirit of truth." A woman struggling with alcoholism states: "I have been sober for 14 months, with reliance on my Higher Power, which I have learned to name the Advocate sent by Jesus. A secretary who loves her Catholic faith testifies: "I have participated in a charismatic prayer group for a number of years and have come to a greater appreciation of the gifts of the Holy Spirit operative in our world today." A successful corporate executive admits: "Many of my good decisions that helped others and served the common good were influenced by my prayers to the Holy Spirit for guidance."

> Can I think of times when the Holy Spirit has been active in my life and how could the Advocate play a larger role in my spirituality?

65. How do I handle the little deaths of life?

Let us reflect on the last and most impressive of the seven signs in John's Gospel, the one that culminates in Jesus raising his good friend Lazarus back to life and includes a remarkable claim originally addressed to Martha and Mary, sisters of Lazarus, and—by extension—to us (John 11: 1-45). In his conversation with Martha, Jesus says "I am the resurrection and the life. Those who believe in me, even though they die, will live, and everyone who lives and believes in me will never die." Since this claim to immortality is obviously not true in a literal sense, we ponder its deeper meaning.

For Christians, Jesus reveals the most significant truths about human existence. His life of commitment to the cause of God brought him to death on the cross, but this total self-giving issued in a new, glorified, risen life that he shares with us. He is indeed the resurrection and the life.

Death in its many guises (sickness, failure, sin, disappointment, limitations) constantly shadows our life journey, until it finally encloses us in total darkness. But death, as revealed by Christ, does not have the final word. It is always surrounded by a more powerful light, encompassed by a more vibrant energy we call grace. The Spirit unleashed by the risen Christ can transform the many deaths that threaten us into new forms of life. As Jesus taught: even if we die, we shall live.

We all know stories that exemplify this truth. At the age of 50, Pete, a hard-driving executive, had a serious heart attack—stopped by God for speeding, as he put it. After surgery and recuperation, Pete made radical changes in his life style: less alcohol and more exercise; less time at work and more time with the family; less attention to his investments and more engagement in daily prayer. Now more composed, integrated, and peaceful than ever before, Pete is extremely grateful to God for transforming his illness into a more satisfying life.

Sarah, married ten years and mother of two, went through a painful divorce that left her with strong feelings of anger and disappointment. Rather than wallow in self-pity, she participated in a divorce support group for a couple of years until she regained her self-confidence. Then she went back to school to finish her education that was interrupted when she got married. Armed with a degree, she was able to get a better job that gave her greater flexibility in managing work and family responsibilities. With the Lord's help, Sarah transformed a divorce that felt like death into a new life filled with meaning and purpose.

The raising of Lazarus is a sign of the presence in the world of God's reign, where grace can transform the many forms of death into new, more fulfilling forms of life. Recalling Lazarus-like stories, our own and others, helps confirm this crucial truth and strengthens our hope that life's journey, always shadowed by death, is ultimately meaningful.

> Can I recall a time when I actually experienced
> the transforming power of God's grace?

66. Do I feel threatened by the evil in the world?

In Matthew's Gospel, we find the parable that likens the kingdom of heaven to a householder who sowed good seed in his field, only to have an enemy come and sow weeds among the wheat (Matthew 13: 24-30). When his slaves ask if they should pull up the weeds, the owner tells them to let them grow together until harvest when they can bundle the weeds for burning and gather the wheat into the barn.

The parables of Jesus typically combine familiar elements with some oddity designed to challenge conventional ways of thinking. In this parable the odd factor is that the householder rejects the common-sense solution to do the weeding right away, opting instead for the impractical plan of letting the wheat and weeds grow together and separating them at harvest time. This oddity prompts reflection on possible meanings of the parable: God's ways are mysterious; God does not intervene to get rid of all the weeds, or evil, in the world; our daily existence is a mix of wheat and weeds, good and evil, positive and negative energy; expecting to get rid of all the weeds now is a utopian dream that can only lead to frustration; we must do all we can to eliminate the weeds now, while realistically accepting their persistence; our Christian hope is that God will ultimately accomplish the total victory of good over evil. We can imagine individuals appropriating aspects of this parable as they struggle with the weeds in their own lives.

A young couple deeply in love entered into marriage expecting to live a happy, trouble-free life together. When the romantic aspect of their love faded and the daily grind of work and child-rearing threatened their relationship, they appropriated the sober message of the parable of the wheat and weeks, becoming more realistic about the challenges of married life and finding ways to deepen their love for each other.

A woman who lost her husband to cancer at a young age went through a long grieving process that transformed her denial, anger, and frustration into a relatively peaceful acceptance of her situation as a widowed single mother. When her anger over her fate suddenly flared up again, she recalled the parable of the persistent weeds and resolved to redo the grieving process relying once again on God's help.

An idealistic single woman, inspired by Catholic social teaching, got involved in working for various peace and justice causes. She found herself dealing with deep misunderstandings, enduring prejudices and even personal attacks. She maintained her commitment by remembering that God does not intervene to remove the weeds but does ultimately reward good efforts.

A woman who was very involved in her parish became deeply

upset by the clergy sex abuse scandal, especially the complicity of some bishops. As she struggled to make sense of the whole sordid mess, the parable of the good and bad seeds reminds her that the Church, far from being a perfect society, remains what it has always been: a graced but sinful institution, where wheat and weeds grow together. This perspective helped her transform her anger at the clergy and hierarchy into positive energy for serving her parish.

> What are my own utopian dreams for a weedless world, and how can I put Gospel realism into practice?

67. How receptive am I to the Word of God?

Matthew tells us the story of the sower who scattered seed that fell ineffectively on the path, rocky ground, and among thorns, but also fell on fertile soil, where it produced fruit up to an incredible hundredfold (Matthew 13: 1-23). After an explanation of why Jesus taught in parables, Matthew adds an allegorical explanation of the original parable of Jesus that invites a self-examination on the obstacles to a more fruitful reception of God's word. By clearing away the obstacles, we put ourselves in a better position to experience the immense power of God's word to spur our spiritual growth. Let us consider some possible examples.

Jason, a middle-aged, practicing Catholic with a tolerable marriage and secure job, had lived his whole adult life with a grade-school understanding of his faith. Recognizing himself in the seed that falls on the path (hearing the word without understanding it), he undertook a study of his Catholic faith that included attending a series of parish sponsored lectures and reading some of the recommended books. As Jason achieved a deeper understanding of his faith, he found that he got more out of Sunday liturgy, related to his wife in a more satisfying way, and found greater meaning in his job. As Isaiah taught, God's word is indeed like the rain and the snow that make the earth fertile and fruitful.

Life was good for Mary, a satisfying career, a happy marriage, two healthy children, a vibrant parish, and an energizing prayer life. Then her teenage son got involved in drugs, initiating a whole series of problems: stealing, juvenile court, rehab program, relapse, health issues. She prayed every day for him, but without apparent effect. Her faith was shaken. She felt like the rocky ground in Matthew's parable, where the seed has no roots and falls away when tribulation comes. Anxious about her crisis of faith, Mary began a daily meditation on Christ's agony in the garden, where he had to deal with the apparent failure of his mission and the weakness of his chosen disciples. Strengthened by this prayerful encounter with Christ, the living Word of God, Mary was able to reappropriate her faith and persevere in the difficult task of loving her son. When God's Word finds fertile ground, it produces amazing fruit.

When John reflected on the seed that fell among thorns and was choked by "worldly anxiety and the lure of riches," he experienced an immediate shock of self-discovery. He had spent his life climbing the corporate ladder. His job was always more important than his family. His vast accumulation of possessions had left him spiritually deprived. Without even recognizing it, he had fallen into a consumerist mentality that links happiness to material goods. Facing the hard truth about the lure of riches flooded John's mind with good intentions: pay more attention to his wife; develop a better relationship with his adult children; simplify his lifestyle; give more money to charity; volunteer to tutor inner city youth. Only time will tell if John turns his good intentions into consistent Christian action. There is no doubt, however, that his good effort will be more than matched by God's abundant grace.

> Do any of the examples above prompt personal reflection on how I could be more receptive to God's powerful word?

68. Do I appreciate the depth dimension of everyday life?

The evangelist Mark reminds us that Jesus used many parables to teach the people about the kingdom of God. In his teaching, Jesus did not propose philosophical arguments or use abstract language but told stories drawing on familiar experiences of ordinary people. His parables were designed to get people to think more deeply about life, to examine common assumptions, to broaden narrow perspectives, to make better moral judgments, and to live as more effective disciples.

For example, Jesus compared the reign of God to seed which takes root and grows apart from the attention or knowledge of the sower (Mark 4: 26-29). One implication of the parable is that God's reign is growing in our world in mysterious ways that we can easily miss as we go about our daily tasks. More is going on in human affairs than meets the eye. God's grace silently accomplishes significant things great and small. The parable challenges us to see the world with eyes of faith, to probe beneath the external appearances of life, to discern the mystery dimension of experience, to try and align ourselves with the direction and dynamics of the kingdom.

We can imagine individuals responding to the parable of the seed. A married couple begins to look for ways to help each other grow spiritually. A corporate executive, long driven by the lure of ever greater financial rewards, decides to redirect her energy into becoming a deeper, more authentic person. After making a marriage encounter, a husband realizes that he cannot read his wife like a book, making her newly mysterious to him. A lifelong Catholic comes to see that going to Mass is not merely an obligation but an opportunity to come closer to Christ. A woman upset with the Church hierarchy looks for signs that Pope Francis is having a positive influence on his fellow bishops. A citizen depressed by the moral deterioration of society consciously looks for and finds some positive trends: lower rates of violent crime; a reduction in sexual promiscuity and abortion; fewer teenage pregnancies; a growing percentage of young people doing volunteer service projects and actively caring for the environment. A veteran deals with depression by helping other veterans who are suffering physically and emotionally.

> How can I deepen and expand my awareness of God's reign secretly growing in our world?

69. Am I aware of signs of hope in my life?

In John's Gospel, Jesus promises his disciples that he will not leave them orphans but will ask the Father to send them the Advocate, the Spirit of truth who will remain with them (John 14: 15-21). The Christian claim is that Christ has kept his promise and that the Holy Spirit lives within us as a source of guidance and hope. This hope is a gift from God, an unmerited blessing, an ultimately ineffable mystery of grace. There is no adequate reason, no purely logical explanation for the gift of hope.

The crucified and risen Christ is himself our hope. As Christians, we see him as the fulfillment of the hopes of Israel for a messiah, the "Anointed One," an enduring son of David, a final prophet who would save the people. Jesus lived a life of complete confidence in God and the divine promises. Despite the darkness of his passion, Jesus continued to trust God, commending his spirit into his Father's care, for which God raised him to life from death. The resurrection, which validated the trust Jesus placed in Abba, stands as the great guarantee for us that God is indeed trustworthy, forever faithful to the divine promises, including the gift of the Advocate.

Jesus taught us to place our hopes in the coming reign of God, which is already present in our world but will be complete only at the end of time. Our faith in the ultimate triumph of God's justice and love enables us to detect signs of hope today. In the preaching of Jesus, the metaphor of the coming kingdom of God includes hope for the salvation both of individuals, who ultimately find fulfillment of their deepest longings, and of the whole of creation, which shares in the victory of God's children.

Christian hope, grounded in Christ and his teaching on the reign of God, is expressed by individual believers in specific statements: "As my body grows weaker, I hope soon to be with God in heaven." "My hope surges when I see the first violets and daffodils of spring." "Despite all the failures, I still hope for peace between Israel and the Palestinians." "As a pure gift, I have this fundamental hope that life makes sense and that my good efforts are worthwhile". "My hope is that all of God's children will be saved." "The dream of a transformed world, with a new heaven and new earth, expands my hope beyond me getting to heaven. My hope for the world gets a boost when I think about all the good people who do charitable work." "With all the bad news circulating around, I need daily prayer and weekly Mass to avoid despair and keep my hopes alive."

> What is my own deepest experience of hope?

70. What are my own deepest spiritual experiences?

In the Gospel of John, we encounter a familiar figure, Thomas, the twin, commonly known today as "Doubting Thomas." He was not with the other disciples when the risen Christ first appeared to them. When the others shared the good news with him, Thomas emphatically declared that he would not believe unless he saw for himself the wounds of the crucified Lord, putting his finger in the nail marks and his hand into Christ's pierced side. Not satisfied with the testimony of others, Thomas wanted to experience the risen Lord himself, to know first-hand that his crucified Master was indeed alive in a new and glorious way.

A week later, Jesus appeared again to the disciples, and this time Thomas was with them. Inviting Thomas to see and touch his wounds, Jesus said, "Do not doubt but believe." Thomas answered with one of the great faith statements in the Gospels: "My Lord and my God!" Jesus then added: "Blessed are those who have not seen and yet have come to believe" (John 20: 19-29).

Thomas represents the contemporary desire for direct religious experience. The traditional supports for belief have been weakened. Atheism is now a viable option in our culture. Young people today do not automatically follow the religious beliefs and traditions of their parents. In this situation, individuals are more likely to appropriate or maintain the Christian faith if they have a genuine experience of God's saving love mediated by Jesus Christ.

A widow who suffered intense feelings of loneliness after her husband's unexpected death came to cope with her new life situation, convinced she would survive only with God's help. A cradle Catholic who kept the commandments throughout his life made a retreat and developed a new personal relationship with Christ, which deepened his faith and expanded his commitment to help those in need. Reflecting on her life, a grandmother realized that she had always felt Christ's presence, especially in the sacraments, leading her to a profound sense of gratitude for the gift of faith. A woman who doubted God's merciful love for years after having an abortion, participated in the American Bishops' national program, Project Rachel, designed to bring healing to those involved in abortion and was blessed with a solid, enduring belief in a merciful God who never tires of forgiving. A young man who lived as a nominal Catholic without much thought or conviction, even when going to Mass and after getting married in the Church, had a great awakening when he held his newborn son in his arms for the first time and spontaneously prayed with Thomas: "My Lord and my God!"

71. How can I find peace when my soul is troubled?

The Gospel of John tells us that the disciples were gathered in a locked room for fear of their fellow Jews. It is Sunday evening, the third day since their Master, Jesus of Nazareth, was apprehended and executed by the Romans. We can imagine something of their mental and emotional state: deeply fearful for their own lives; completely dispirited, since they had hoped that Jesus was the Messiah who would save them; horribly guilty for running away when Jesus was arrested and needed their support; and totally confused about what they would do next. Suddenly, Jesus is in their midst, proclaiming: "Peace be with you." Then he shows them the wounds in his hands and his side and repeats, "Peace be with you." Jesus does not berate them for their lack of faith or chastise them for their cowardice but simply offers them a greeting which conveys understanding, love, and forgiveness. After repeating his greeting of peace, Jesus breathed upon the disciples and declared: "Receive the Holy Spirit. If you forgive the sins of any, they are forgiven them; if you retain the sins of any, they are retained" (John 20: 19-23).

We all know something of the fear, hopelessness, guilt, and confusion experienced by the disciples after the death of Jesus, and some of us can testify to the transforming power of Christ's peace and the gift of the Spirit. After suffering a heart attack, Sam, an engineer who had little experience of fear throughout his life, became surprisingly anxious about many things, especially death. Feeling weak and vulnerable, he read about Cardinal Joseph Bernardin, who dealt with his terminal cancer by "befriending death."

Sam began praying every day that Christ would breathe the Holy Spirit upon him to help him befriend death. Over time he found that the more he was able to accept death as part of life, the better he was able to manage his daily fears.

Donna, who suffered an unwanted divorce just two years into her marriage, was disheartened and cynical about life in general and men in particular. Nevertheless, she continued to participate in the liturgy, receiving communion every Sunday. Donna joined a support group for divorced persons sponsored by her parish and once a week tutored a first-grade girl in an inner-city school. After a couple of years, she was able to express more positive personal thoughts and feelings: "I can still have a fulfilling life; I must learn to forgive those who hurt me, including my ex-husband; I see now that Christ's peace is more powerful than the cynicism that threatened to poison my soul; I am learning to trust the Holy Spirit to guide and strengthen me as I get on with the often confusing task of making a better life for myself and others."

> Have I experienced Christ's peace and the gift of the Spirit in my own life?

72. What does the Lord's Prayer mean to me?

Evidently impressed with the prayer life of their Master and seeking guidance like the Baptist gave to his followers, the disciples ask Jesus to teach them to pray. In Luke's Gospel, Jesus responds with what we know as the Lord's Prayer: "Father, hallowed be your name. Your kingdom come. Give us each day our daily bread. And forgive us our sins, for we ourselves forgive everyone indebted to us. And do not bring us to the time of trial" (Luke 11: 1-4). We, of course, are more familiar with Matthew's embellished version, but the fundamental pattern is the same. As disciples of Jesus, we are blessed to follow his example and address God as

Father, our translation of the Aramaic "Abba" used by children to address their father. The God we address in prayer loves us unconditionally, always ready to forgive. In prayer, we lift our minds and hearts to God as the transcendent judge of all. We also engage in familiar prayerful conversation with the God who lives within us as the Source of our drive for love and knowledge. By praying that God's name be hallowed, we recognize our obligation to offer praise and adoration to our Creator and Judge.

Keeping in mind our total dependence on Abba, we are free to put our petitions before the gracious God. Preparing for the coming of the kingdom is the fundamental request that God's reign will finally be achieved and that we will participate in the process here and now. Asking for daily bread reminds us that God is the continuing source of all gifts that satisfy our human needs. Jesus links God's forgiveness of us to our forgiveness of others, not as earning divine mercy but as opening our hearts to the free gift of a fresh start. When we pray "do not bring us to the time of trial," we are also asking for divine help to overcome the temptations that assail us on the journey of life.

Individuals who reflect on Luke's less familiar version of the Lord's Prayer can develop healthier Christian attitudes and practices. A woman who typically views God as a harsh disciplinarian like her father, comes to see God more as a compassionate loving presence like her mother. A hard-driving advertising man who made a successful career his highest priority sees the light and makes a radical conversion, redirecting his energy to spreading God's reign in his own family. An accountant who always asked God for favors in his prayers starts offering more prayers praising God's name. A grandmother who was reluctant to offer too many petitioning prayers now feels comfortable asking very specific blessings for each of her ten grandchildren. A married man long addicted to gambling becomes more confidant that God will give him strength to meet the test and kick his dangerous habit.

73. How important is God's kingdom in my life?

"The kingdom of heaven is like a merchant searching for fine pearls. When he finds a pearl of great price, he goes and sells all that he has and buys it" (Matthew 13: 45-46). This verse prompts personal reflection on what we treasure. What is the pearl of great price for *me*? What excites *my* interests or stirs *my* passions? For what am *I* willing to sacrifice?

The parable suggests that the pearl of great price is the kingdom of heaven, also called the reign of God. The image of the kingdom, with its roots in the Hebrew Scriptures, was central in the teaching of Jesus. Where God reigns there is peace and justice. When kingdom ideals prevail, individuals—empowered by divine love—enjoy personal fulfillment, form mutually beneficial relationships, and participate in vibrant, supportive communities. In the teaching of Jesus, the kingdom is already here, present in the hearts of individuals and in humane structures of the world, but it will be complete only at the end of time when God is all in all.

To treasure the kingdom is to commit ourselves to the cause of God and humanity. Doing God's will is the pearl of great price, worthy of self-sacrifice. Spreading the reign of God in the world deserves our best efforts. Confidence in the ultimate fulfillment of the kingdom helps sustain our dedication to the cause. Yet we all know the temptation to substitute our will for God's will; to make worldly matters into ultimate concerns; to skew our priorities; and to lose focus on kingdom ideals.

In managing this temptation, we might ask God for the gift of wisdom, as did King Solomon, who requested an understanding heart that could distinguish right from wrong. The gift of wisdom can direct us to concrete, practical ways to keep our priorities in proper order. Some examples: a busy, ambitious father sets aside generous blocks of time to be attentive to each of his three children; a couple preparing the family budget starts first of all by setting aside substantial amounts for church and charities; a woman with a demanding job gets up early and does a half-hour of spiritual reading and meditation before going to work; a big baseball fan, who would like to watch all the games on television, purposely limits her viewing in order to talk to her husband about deeper matters.

> What specific step could I take to keep my focus on God's kingdom?

74. Which person of the Trinity is most important to me?

In his "Farewell Discourse" recorded in John's Gospel, Jesus speaks of the "Spirit of truth," who will "guide you into all the truth" while reminding his disciples of his close relationship to the Father. This passage reminds us of the Trinitarian character of Christian spirituality, which recognizes the threefold way we experience the one God, as Father, Son and Holy Spirit.

For example, Sue, a grad student in pharmacy, feels loved by the God she likes to call "Father." She believes that the Father created her in love, calls her by name, and has a plan for her life. Most days she spends a few minutes talking to the Father in her own familiar words, confident that God hears her. When discouraged and confused, Denise asks God to hold her in his strong and gracious arms, often finding comfort in this intimate embrace.

Frank, a hard-working truck driver, has a very Christ-centered spirituality. He senses that Jesus listens to him when he talks to him like a good friend. He finds inspiration in the Gospel stories that portray Jesus casting out demons and forgiving sinners. Last Palm Sunday, he got teary when he heard in the Passion the part about Jesus feeling abandoned on the cross. Frank does not often speak openly about his relationship with Christ, but his family recognizes by his actions how important the Lord is in his life.

Beth, a senior member of a religious order, has recently been made more aware of the activity of the Holy Spirit in her life. As she looks back now, she is more conscious of how the Spirit has guided her through crucial decisions that confronted her throughout her life. It is as though the Holy Spirit has been a light unto her path. Her prayer has now become less wordy and more receptive to the subtle promptings of the Spirit. She often uses what she calls "Spirit language" to speak about the mission of the Church because it sounds more open and inclusive.

> Which person of the Trinity most influences my own spirituality? Why? How?

Chapter Four

Christology (following Jesus, Our Friend)

75. Who is Christ for me?

Luke tells us that Jesus, after praying in solitude, asks his disciples who the crowds think he is. They reply that some say John the Baptist, others Elijah, or one of the ancient prophets who has died. Then Jesus puts to the disciples a personal question: "But who do you say that I am?" As the spokesperson for the group, Peter responds: "The Messiah of God" indicating that Jesus is the anointed one promised by God and the long-awaited Messiah now sent by God. Jesus then directs them not to tell anyone, perhaps because others would think he was a political leader who would free them from the Roman yoke. After predicting his passion, death, and resurrection at the hands of the religious leaders, Jesus tells his followers to deny themselves and take up the cross daily: "For those who want to save their life will lose it, and those who lose their life for my sake will save it" (Luke 9: 18-24).

We can hear the Gospel as an invitation to respond personally to the question: "Who do you say that I am?" We know the answer has practical consequences, that following Christ means taking up the cross on a daily basis. Traditionally, Christians have affirmed that Jesus Christ is both true God (one in being with the Father as the Nicene Creed puts it) and true human (like us in all things but sin). Within that broad framework, some have emphasized the divinity of Christ, others his humanity. Some believers focus on the passion and death of Jesus on the cross, others on his resurrection and ongoing presence. There is always the danger of distorting the real Jesus by making him into a projection of our own needs or a defender of our bias: for example, turning him into a warrior who supports war and violence, or a tribal leader who justifies racial superiority.

More specifically, faithful individuals today have their own ways of identifying Jesus. A dedicated lawyer sees Christ as the greatest ethical teacher, providing a moral compass as he works his way through complex ethical issues. A grandmother who has buried a husband and a daughter views Jesus as her companion on the journey through the dark valley, one who always hears her cries for help. An electrician serious about understanding his faith, thinks of Jesus as the supreme teacher, patient with slow learners. A religious sister feels closer to God now that she understands Christ as the cosmic Lord who is the energy and the goal of the whole 13-billion-year evolutionary process. A teacher who is struggling with serious doubts about the divinity of Christ hangs onto his conviction that Jesus is the best guide to a fulfilled life of service to others.

> What step could I take to make Christ more significant in my life?

76. How can I become a more compassionate person?

In Luke's Gospel, Jesus, with his disciples and a large crowd, meets a funeral procession as he enters the city of Nain. Moved with pity, he says to the widow burying her only son: "Do not weep." Then touching the coffin, he says: "Young man, I say to you, rise!" The dead man sits up and begins to speak and Jesus gives him to his mother. Seized with fear, the crowd glorifies God, exclaiming: "A great prophet has risen among us," and "God has looked favorably on his people" (Luke 7: 11-17).

With the help of biblical scholars, we can learn a great deal about Jesus from this wondrous story. Evidently, he carried out his mission by travelling from city to city in his home area of Galilee. His preaching of the kingdom and his miraculous cures attracted large crowds as his fame spread. When Jesus saw the widow, he "had compassion for her," the Greek word suggesting a deep visceral response to the plight of a woman who is not only grieving the loss of her son but also faces a difficult and dangerous social situation with no man to look out for her. Jesus is a human being like us with deep emotions—including compassion for those suffering. In this case, his empathy moved him to quick and decisive action, raising the young man to life without even a request from his mother. In this sense, the miracle is highly unusual, since in most cases Jesus shared his healing power only with persons who sought his help because they had faith in him.

Jesus was indeed a miracle worker, as even his opponents admitted. His marvelous deeds, however, were not designed to call attention to himself but to manifest the presence and character of God's reign in the world. In and through Jesus, God did indeed visit his people. The crowd got it right when they proclaimed Jesus a great prophet. He stands in the line of both Elijah and Elisha, who each restored dead sons to life. As Moses prophesized, he is the final prophet sent by God to save the people. He is the Son of God who himself will be raised from the dead by his Father.

We can imagine individuals responding to this gospel passage with a personal comment. One young mother: "I am a person of very strong emotions, which often feels like a curse, but it helps me realize that Jesus himself had deep emotions." A woman religious sister who is dying of cancer: "I ask the Lord to be compassionate toward me, as he was to the grieving mother in Luke's story." A deacon: "I want to be more aware of the people in my community who, like the widows in the biblical period, are banished to the margins, left unprotected, subject to systemic injustices." The deacon's wife talks easily about her personal relationship with Christ: "I understand justice better by reflecting on the very human reactions of Jesus to the widow." A lay minister to prison inmates: "I find support in Jesus, the liberator of captives, who continues to work for the cause of God and humanity."

> What is the most important thing I can learn
> from Jesus about compassion?

77. Where can I find light in the midst of darkness?

The Gospel according to John contains the popular passage, "For God so loved the world that he gave his only Son, so that everyone who believes in him may not perish but may have eternal life" (John 3: 16). The passage goes on to characterize the only Son as the light that "has come into the world, and people loved darkness rather than light because their deeds were evil." John's Gospel sees human existence as an ongoing struggle between light and darkness—between the God of light, most clearly manifested in the fight between Christ, the light of the world, and the dark forces that resist the truth and lead to sin. Given this choice, as we all know from our own experience, it is possible to prefer the darkness to the light.

Preferring darkness takes many forms: habitual sin that is not ready for repentance; willful ignorance that passes up opportunities to learn; entrenched prejudice that is mired in stereotyping; destructive addictions that refuse treatment; and a persistent victimhood that wallows in self-pity.

Christ the light, who has come to save the world, claims power to reveal the darkness, to unmask its deceit, and to replace it with the truth of the Gospel that illumines human existence. We can choose the light, if we accept God's grace. For example, a married man admits that his attraction to a female friend is hurting his marriage and commits himself, with Christ's help, to direct his sexual energy to pleasing his wife. A biology professor recognizes that her grade-school knowledge of her Catholic faith is insufficient and undertakes an informal study of contemporary theology. An assembly-line worker who grew up with a strong bias against blacks, Asians, and Hispanics tries to see Christ in all his co-workers as a way of overcoming the darkness of prejudice. A corporate executive admits that excessive drinking is clouding her judgment and hurting her job performance and begins the practice of saying a prayer on the way to business lunches and dinners, asking Christ for the strength to control her alcohol consumption. A man who has spent two years feeling sorry for himself after a painful divorce realizes he has to leave behind the darkness of self-pity and embrace a future illumined by Christ.

> What darkness impedes my spiritual growth and how can I rely more on Christ, who invites me to embrace the light of truth?

78. Am I attuned to the voice of the Good Shepard?

In John's Gospel, we encounter Jesus as the Good Shepherd, a familiar and comforting image that still resonates with many Christians today. It brings to mind the Shepherd who leads us to still waters, restores our soul, and leads us in right paths (see Psalm 23). The Good Shepherd is especially attentive to those who are lost, leaving the 99 sheep to search for the one stray (Matthew 18:12-14). Jesus, claiming to be one with the Father, declares: "My sheep hear my voice. I know them, and they follow me. I give them eternal life, and they will never perish" (John 10: 27-30). Jesus has a close personal relationship with his followers, promising them the gift of God's saving grace now and forever. His followers are attuned to his voice, open to his message, and dedicated to observing his commands.

Christ the Good Shepherd continues to lead his flock today. His voice can be heard resounding in and through various sources: the Scriptures, the liturgy, the Christian tradition, Church teaching, historical developments, cultural trends, and common human experience. In the contemporary world, Christ's voice competes for attention with the demands of daily life, secular ideologies, and destructive cultural trends such as hedonism, consumerism, racism, and sexism. Given the complexity of our world, it is often difficult to identify Christ's voice and to interpret it properly. Applying Christ's message to concrete situations requires prudent discernment, which all too often falls short of certitude.

Nevertheless, as Christians we must try to be attuned to the voice of the Good Shepherd. This means, in general terms, that Christ and his message have decisive influence on our civic lives. The cross is always judge of the flag. We are first Christians and then Americans. We pledge allegiance first to the Lord and then to the nation. The Christian tradition provides the fundamental framework for judging all cultural trends and societal developments.

We can imagine Christians who have become more attuned to the voice of the Good Shepherd. A woman with a promising career turns down a promotion so she can have more time for her family. An architect who for years refused to listen to anything the bishops say about peace and justice looks for their guidance in applying Catholic social teaching to current issues, such as immigration reform. A grandmother who most of her life thought of Sunday Mass as a time for private prayer now enjoys participating in the liturgy, which reminds her to be more attentive to those in need throughout her life. A veteran who supported the Iraq War thinks he should have paid more attention to the pope who opposed it than to the president who initiated it. A mother who struggled to deal with her rebellious teenage daughter finds a few minutes each day for silent prayer, seeking guidance from the Lord.

> What message does the Good Shepherd have for me?

79. Do I honor Christ as my king?

According to Luke's Passion account, as Jesus is dying on the cross the rulers sneer at him and the soldiers jeer him: "If you are the King of the Jews, save yourself." Above Jesus there was an inscription, "This is the King of the Jews." One of the criminals crucified with Jesus also reviles him, but the other, admitting his guilt, asks the innocent Jesus to remember him when he comes into his kingdom. Jesus replies with comforting words: "Truly I tell you, today you will be with me in Paradise" (Luke 23: 35-43).

The crucifixion scene is paradoxical. Jesus was mocked by the Jewish leaders and Roman soldiers for being who he really was, the chosen one, the Christ of God and King of the Jews. He demonstrated his kingly authority throughout his life by curing the sick, exorcising demons, reconciling sinners, calming the storm, proclaiming divine truth, and confronting authorities. On the cross, Jesus once again exercises his royal authority by promising the repentant criminal the gift of salvation.

Christians today can demonstrate their belief in the kingship of Christ in various ways. A small business owner tries to put Christian principles into practice not only in her family setting but also at the worksite. A father of two teenagers prays every day on the way home from work that Christ the Lord will help him to deal effectively with the unique personalities of each of his children. During the election cycle, a pastor reminds his parishioners that Christ should rule over the political world as well as their personal lives. A checkout clerk in a grocery store tries to treat Muslim women with special respect because she believes Christ the King died and rose for all people.

> In what ways does Christ function as my king, and how can I extend his rule in my life?

80. Am I ever amazed by Christ's grace?

In the first chapter of his Gospel, Mark emphasizes the way Jesus taught: not like the Scribes who offered their opinion based on previous teachings but like the "Holy One of God," who teaches with great personal authority. Mark does not tell us what Jesus said when he took his turn teaching in the Capernaum synagogue, but reports the amazement of the people who heard him proclaim "a new teaching with authority." Their amazement was intensified when Jesus exorcised a man in the synagogue with an unclean spirit, manifesting his power even over the demons (Mark 1: 21-28).

Throughout his public ministry, Jesus taught with absolute authority. "I say to you" was the characteristic way he introduced his reinterpretations of traditional teaching. He presented himself as one who knows the secrets of the Father and shares them with the people. His followers perceived him as an authentic teacher, who lived what he taught. He made a great impact on those who encountered him, typically forcing a decision for or against him.

For us today, Christ remains the Word of God made flesh, the embodiment of divine truth, the manifestation of Divine Wisdom, the parable of the Father. He confronts us as the one who speaks words of eternal life. In a world filled with competing ideologies, Christ claims our allegiance as the authentic guide to full human development. Christ's grace is truly amazing, his teaching astonishing in its authority.

Throughout Christian history great saints have expressed their amazement at Christ and the power of his teaching: for example, Augustine was emotionally overwhelmed by the liberating power of Christ's forgiveness and Teresa of Avila was so taken with Christ's powerful presence in her life that she described it as a "spiritual marriage."

Today, good Christians continue to express amazement at the power of Christ at work in their lives. A recent widow is grateful that Christ helped her get through the Christmas season without being totally overwhelmed by sadness. A truck driver recognizes that only with the Lord's help has he been sober for five years. A young women is surprised when her emotionally abusive father, who experienced Christ's grace in confession, opened up a conversation with her asking for forgiveness. A busy executive is sure that her brief prayer to Christ each morning has reduced her stress level at work. A factory worker notices that his effort to see Christ in his work colleagues has made his job less tedious and more meaningful.

> Do these examples of Christian amazement trigger any responses in my own mind and heart?

81. Where can I find help to bear the burdens of life?

According to Matthew, Jesus addresses a comforting word to all who are burdened, including ourselves (Matthew 11: 25-30). We all know times and ways that life seems burdensome. A father of three, who works two jobs to support his family, feels worn out from his labors. A single mother is overwhelmed with the responsibility of caring for her autistic daughter. A collegian is feeling the pressure of getting into a good graduate program. A husband wonders how long he can continue to care effectively for his wife suffering from dementia. A wife who had an affair is burdened with intense guilt feelings. A woman with a promising career has insomnia and suffers from sleep deprivation.

As we ponder our own distinctive burdens, we hear the comforting words of Christ: "Come to me, all you that are weary and are carrying heavy burdens, and I will give you rest. Take my yoke upon you, and learn from me; for I am gentle and humble in heart, and you will find rest for your souls. For my yoke is easy, and my burden is light." We can deal better with our burdens by joining ourselves to Christ, adopting his mindset, and participating in his mission. As he walked this earth, Jesus knew the burden of physical suffering, emotional distress, and spiritual darkness. He embraced these burdens as byproducts of his fidelity to the will of his Father and his own mission to spread the reign of God in the world.

Belief in Christ does not automatically dissolve our burdens or magically make them disappear. It can, however, lighten them in significant ways: encouraging us to find needed help in carrying them; reminding us that others carry burdens, some heavier than our own; accepting suffering as part of the human condition; finding inspiration in the example of Jesus; and drawing on the strength of Christ's spirit through personal and liturgical prayer.

To take one example, Lee, the single mother of an autistic daughter, responded to the Gospel invitation of Christ by spending ten minutes every day in prayerful meditation, seeking guidance and strength from the Lord. In prayer, she recognized her need for help and joined a support group that put her in touch with other parents of autistic children. The group experience has reminded her she is not alone in the struggle to be a responsible mother and that some parents are carrying crosses heavier than her own. Lee finds that the more she follows the example of Christ by graciously accepting her situation, the more energy she has for loving her daughter and attending to her special needs. Christ, as promised, does indeed lighten burdens, often working through other people.

Can I think of a time when Christ lightened my burden? When? Where? How?

82. Am I open to the healing power of Christ?

In Mark's Gospel, a woman afflicted with hemorrhages for twelve years approaches Jesus from behind and touches his cloak, believing that merely touching his clothes will heal her. Immediately she knows she is cured, and the hemorrhaging stops. Jesus, realizing power has gone out from him, asks his disciples who touched his clothes. The woman then approaches Jesus and tells him the whole story, drawing his response: "Daughter your faith has made you well" (Mark 5: 25-34).

This unnamed, long-suffering woman, who has probably exhausted her financial resources seeking medical help, is indeed a remarkable example of faith. With total trust in the healing power of Jesus, she boldly breaks social and religious prohibitions, approaching him in public and touching his cloak. Her reward is instant healing.

The Gospel reveals Jesus as the Divine Physician, more powerful than the medical doctors. For us, Christ is a living resource of healing power, an always available reservoir of therapeutic energy. He stands ready to heal us in all dimensions of our lives: physically, emotionally, and spiritually. We can encounter his healing touch in the sacraments of Penance and Anointing of the Sick, as well as in the struggles of daily life. As the Gospel instructs us, it is through faith that we can tap the always available healing power of Christ.

Consider these two composite stories of faith healing. A

young woman spent most of her collegiate years in the hook-up culture: friends with benefits, promiscuous sex without commitment, physical intimacy without romance. The whole experience, however, left her feeling guilty and empty. In that state, she met a wonderful guy with high moral standards who really cared for her. Unable to respond fully to his initiatives because of her guilt feelings, she made an appointment with a priest to do a face-to-face confession. She told her whole story and with the prayer of absolution felt the healing power of Christ granting her a new beginning. Feeling better about herself, she followed the advice of the priest and told her boyfriend about her past, which cleared the way for an honest relationship that eventually led to a mutually enriching marriage.

A middle-age man with a loving family and a good job periodically erupted in angry outbursts, sometimes at work but more often at home. Being a man of faith, he turned to Christ in prayer, asking for help to control his temper, and his prayer led him to take an anger management seminar that provided him with some practical advice (such as think before you speak, exercise to reduce stress, and be ready to forgive the offenses of others). Relying on daily prayer, which inspired him to follow these practical strategies, he was able to manage his anger much more effectively.

> Can I think of a time when I felt the healing power of Christ? What happened?

83. How do I deal with my personal demons?

Early in his Gospel, Mark presents Jesus as a healer who cures Peter's mother-in-law of a fever and as an exorcist who casts out demons (Mark 1: 29-39). More than the other evangelists, Mark recounts instances where Jesus demonstrates his power over the demonic forces, typically with just a simple command to leave the possessed individual. During the ministry of Jesus and his early followers, people commonly believed that evil spirits roamed the world causing havoc and harming people. By exorcising the malevolent spirits, Jesus extends the reign of God, bringing proper order into the lives of many people suffering from demonic possession. The demons know who Jesus is, but cannot resist his healing power.

Today, educated people are more likely to think of demonic forces in terms of oppressive social systems and internal impulses to act in destructive ways. The demons causing harm in our world include racism, sexism, and consumerism, as well as pride, lust, and sloth. As contemporary Christians, we are strengthened by the traditional conviction that Christ, the great exorcist, is more powerful than all the dark forces that assail us. In difficult times, it may appear the evil spirits are defeating our best efforts. The good news is, however, that we do not fight the demons alone, but that Christ is with us in the struggle, assuring the final victory of good over evil.

We know Christians who rely on Christ in the struggle for personal integrity and social justice. A married man, who names his demon "lust," says extra prayers to the Lord when he is travelling that he will withstand temptations to infidelity. A woman unsuccessfully fighting the glass ceiling in her company vows to continue the struggle after reflecting on the amazing power of Jesus over demonic forces. A parish social justice committee, feeling very discouraged about continuing racial tensions in their community, recommit themselves to the cause of racial justice after hearing a talk on Jesus as exorcist in Mark's Gospel. A collegian with high intelligence and low motivation names his demon "laziness" and asks Christ's help to work harder on his studies. An affluent couple, long dominated by the demonic power of consumerism, decides to take initial steps to simplify their lifestyle after reading a homily by Pope Francis on Christ, friend of the poor.

> What demonic force concerns me the most, and how can I best enlist Christ's help in the struggle?

84. Where do I find joy in my life?

The evangelist John records seven signs or miracles performed by Jesus. In the first sign Jesus, along with his mother and his disciples, is at a wedding feast in Cana of Galilea. His mother (she is never named in John's Gospel) tells him: "They have no wine." Jesus seems to put her off: "Woman, what concern is that to you and to me? My hour has not yet come." But then, responding to his mother's request, he orders the servants to fill six stone water jugs, holding twenty to thirty gallons filled to the brim, and to take some of the water—now turned to wine—to the headwaiter, who says to the bridegroom that everyone serves the good wine first but, "you have kept the good wine until now" (John 2: 1-11). The evangelist then tells us that this first sign revealed the glory of Jesus and his disciples began to believe in him.

For us today, the Cana story, rich in symbolism, reminds us of some of the fundamental claims of our Christian faith: Jesus is the Son of God sent into the world to inaugurate a new era of divine blessing; his glory initially manifested at Cana was fully revealed in his supreme hour of glory when he was lifted up on the cross; through his death and resurrection he sent the Holy Spirit to all of us as a super abundant resource that is always renewable and never runs out; he set the stage for a community that could rejoice in his continuing presence.

There are people who know from experience the spiritual truths suggested by the sign performed at Cana. A convert to Catholicism, who went through the RCIA program, loves participating in the liturgy, which has an amazing power to lift her spirits and gladden her heart. A middle-age couple did a Marriage Encounter that brought new life to their marriage and revealed unrecognized gifts in each other. A married woman who was having an affair with her boss broke it off, went to confession, and felt like a new person with a clean slate and a fresh opportunity to form a more satisfying relationship with her husband. A youth minister, who read the apostolic exhortation by Pope Francis *The Joy of the Gospel* is very excited about sharing such an uplifting presentation of the Christian faith with her students.

Have I experienced the uplifting power of Christ's grace, and how could I share this gift with others?

85. Do I have faith in the healing power of Christ?

Luke tells the story of a Roman centurion who sends Jewish elders to Jesus asking him to come and save the life of his dying slave. Encouraged by the elders, who point out that the centurion loves the Jewish people and built the synagogue for them in Capernaum, Jesus heads for his house. Before he gets there, however, the centurion, a man accustomed to having his orders obeyed, sends word to Jesus that he does not feel worthy to have him enter his house "but only speak the word, and let my servant be healed." Amazed at this, Jesus tells the crowd: "I tell you, not even in Israel have I found such faith" (Luke 7: 1-10). When the messengers returned to the house, they found the slave in good health.

The unnamed centurion is a remarkable figure. He was a soldier in the mighty Roman army that ruled Israel with an iron hand; and yet the Jewish people thought of him as a friend who had gone out of his way to facilitate their worship. As an officer in charge of 100 soldiers, he had a slave, which made him complicit in the whole cruel institution of slavery; and yet he demonstrated great concern for his dying servant. Based just on word of mouth, he had a deep faith that Jesus could cure his slave. He addressed Jesus as "Lord," which was a title of respect and could express religious belief. He showed a certain humility when he said he was not worthy to have Jesus enter his house. Furthermore, the centurion, who functioned within a system of strict authority, had no doubt that Jesus could simply say the word and heal his servant. Impressed with the man's great faith, Jesus granted his request.

We can envision positive responses to the good example of the Roman centurion today. A man who runs a resort hotel vows to treat his immigrant employees with greater respect. A woman makes her petitionary prayers more open-ended, without trying to tell God exactly how to help people. A collegian tries to put more meaning into the prayer said at Mass right before going to communion, reflecting especially on the power of Christ to heal his unworthy soul. A white teacher, newly conscious of how she has been blessed in life, commits herself to being extra attentive to minority students.

> What can I learn from the story of the Roman centurion?

86. Am I prepared to meet Christ in my life?

In Luke's Gospel, Jesus tells his disciples to prepare for the coming of the Son of Man, who may arrive at an unexpected hour. They are to be like servants who await their master's return from a wedding banquet, well prepared to open the door for him whenever he arrives, even late into the night. Appreciative of their vigilance, he will fasten his belt, have them sit down to eat, and will come and serve them (Luke 12: 35-40).

We can interpret the Gospel as a call to be prepared for the coming of Christ—not only at the end of time but also in our daily lives. We are to be on alert for any word from the Lord that comes to us in and through special moments of grace as well as in and through our everyday experiences. Prepared by prayer and reflection, our task is to discern the authentic voice of Christ and to respond to his personal call.

A composite story to illustrate the Gospel's emphasis on being prepared. A young couple, Abby and James, deeply in love took very seriously their responsibility to prepare for a happy, challenging Christian marriage. They participated wholeheartedly in the parish marriage preparation program: meeting three times with the priest who would marry them; filling out a questionnaire that prompted serious discussion on their quite different attitudes toward spending money; participating in a whole day of guided discussion led by married couples on various aspects of marriage such as communication, sexuality, and spirituality. They made a mutual decision to exercise restraint in their sexual relationship, saving intercourse for marriage. This led them to search for other ways to enjoy one another's company. Although their interests were different (sports for him and music for her), they found a mutual love for nature (walking in the metro park, gardening, spending time by the water). They wanted their marriage ceremony to be a spiritual event and not a show. With this in mind, they spent a good deal of prayerful time choosing the scripture readings and writing a commentary on them which the priest used in preparing his homily. Before the wedding, they experimented with various ways of praying together, finding that it worked best if they actually set aside time to read a passage from the Bible and discuss something that struck them.

Reflecting now on their first ten years of marriage, they can see that their preparation attuned them to the presence of Christ in their shared life together. Their love making feels graced, bringing them closer to each other and to the Lord. Their regular prayer together helps them through difficult times. Their shared enjoyment of nature renews their spirits. They are grateful that their spiritual approach to marriage has enriched them both individually and as a couple. They prepared well and have been blessed with Christ's presence in their marriage.

> How can I better prepare for encountering Christ in my life?

87. How can I manage the storms of life?

Matthew's Gospel, we encounter the impetuous flawed leader of the Twelve, Simon Peter. He is in a boat with the other disciples when a storm comes up. Jesus then appears, walking on the water. When Peter realizes it is Jesus and not a ghost, he, at the Lord's invitation, begins walking on the water toward Jesus. But noticing the storm's strong wind, he becomes frightened and cries out Lord save me. Jesus catches Peter and says: "You of little faith, why did you doubt?" (Matthew 14:22-33).

Peter was doing well when he was intent on reaching Jesus, but he faltered when his attention was diverted to the storm. This incident suggests a "Spiritual Peter Principle:" When the storms of life threaten us, it is wise to concentrate more on the saving presence of Christ than on the dangers of the storms.

We all know something of the traumatic storms that can threaten our lives: the death of a loved one; contracting a serious illness; an unwelcomed divorce; the loss of a job; the breakup of a friendship; betrayal by a colleague. We also know milder storms that cloud our relationships: a misunderstanding with a friend; a spat with a spouse; a disappointment with a child; an argument with an associate. When such experiences dominate our attention, we may suffer a loss of energy and an increase in anxiety.

Faced with storms, we do better to concentrate our attention on the person and power of Christ. One way of doing this is by attending to daily prayer, regular meditation, spiritual reading and weekly liturgy. We can also be attentive to the Lord by concentrating on participating in his mission to spread the kingdom: for example, loving our neighbor; supporting good causes; and caring for those in need. Keeping our attention on Christ and his mission helps us maintain perspective on the storms that can all too easily generate a paralyzing anxiety and self-pity.

We can learn from individuals who have kept their focus on Christ in order to weather the storms of life. A woman diagnosed with breast cancer keeps a positive attitude by meditating on the healing miracles of Jesus. A man who lost his job volunteers regularly at a food distribution center, which keeps him from feeling sorry for himself and motivates him to keep searching for a new job. A widower, who went into a deep depression when his wife died suddenly, begins to feel more like himself as he gets more involved in his parish.

The Spiritual Peter Principle contains a wisdom that can help all of us better manage the inevitable storms that threaten our inner peace and emotional equilibrium by keeping our eyes on Christ and participating in his mission to spread the reign of God in the world.

> Can I think of a way Christ has helped me cope
> when threatened by a storm?

88. What are my most intense spiritual hungers?

In the sixth chapter of John's Gospel, Jesus tries to get the crowd to reflect on the deeper significance of the remarkable sign they just experienced when he fed the multitude with a few loaves of bread. After admonishing the people to work not for perishable food but for food that endures, Jesus responds to their request for this food by saying: "I am the bread of life. Whoever comes to me will never be hungry, and whoever believes in me will never be thirsty" (John 6: 25-35).

This passage prompts reflection on our own deeper hungers: for a comprehensive meaning that enables us to manage the crosses of life; for an overarching purpose that helps make sense of our daily routine; for an imperishable love that satisfies the longings of the heart; for a centered identity that holds despite stress and frustration; for a wholehearted commitment that keeps us engaged in the cause of justice and peace.

As we reflect on our own spiritual hungers, we are encouraged and guided by the Gospel assurance that Christ is the one sent by God, the bread of life, the Lord who satisfies our deepest hungers.

We can imagine individuals offering personal testimony to the nourishing power of Christ. "My faith in Christ, who knew the rejection of friends, kept me from getting bitter during a difficult divorce." "Learning more about how each of the Gospels portrays Jesus has helped satisfy my need to be an intellectually honest Christian." "Christ's identification of himself with the hungry and thirsty has enabled me to maintain my commitment to serve the poor." "Regular meditation on the life of Christ has strengthened my fundamental identity as a Christian disciple." "Our shared faith in Christ has encouraged us to make a better marriage that is mutually nourishing."

> How has Christ satisfied my deepest hungers?

89. How does the Eucharist nourish my soul?

In the United States today, we continue to see widespread interest in spirituality. Our consumerist culture, with its great emphasis on acquiring material goods, often leaves the spirit undernourished, hungering for a life filled with deeper meaning, larger purpose, and greater commitment: a middle-age widow longs for personal intimacy; a wealthy man who has indulged all of his physical desires now feels an intense need to feed his soul; a poor woman who found a job feels blessed and longs to help others seeking employment; a doctor who works long hours comes to Mass on Sunday looking for something to chew on during the week. Spiritual hungers are all too easily eclipsed in our secular culture. It may take prayerful reflection to discern our own dominate hunger.

The Bread of Life Discourse in John's Gospel indicates that Jesus himself is our spiritual nourishment, the one who can satisfy our spiritual hungers. In words that remind us of the Eucharist, Jesus declares: "For the bread of God is that which comes down from heaven and gives life to the world" (John 6: 22-58). Eating this bread unites us to Christ, who gives us the gift of eternal life to enjoy already on this earth. Just as Jesus has life because of the Father who sent him, so we who feed on Christ have life because of him. Feeding on Christ in the Eucharist helps us recognize the ways Christ nourishes us in our daily lives, as these composite examples suggest.

Sam's spiritual hunger is for greater personal development. His passion is to be a more authentic, integrated, faithful Christian disciple. His strategy is to mine the riches of the Liturgy of the Word at Sunday Mass. During the week, he spends time prayerfully reflecting on the Sunday readings with the help of a commentary that provides background for each of the scripture readings. With this preparation, Sam finds that on most Sundays he can hear a word from the Lord, spoken through a scripture verse or a comment in the homily, that nourishes his soul and helps satisfy his hunger to be a better disciple of Christ.

Barbara's spiritual hunger has a strong communal dimension. Her passion is for greater intimacy in her marriage, deeper relationships with her friends, and closer cooperation with colleagues at work. She loves participating in the Sunday liturgy at her local parish, where she feels at home and experiences a deep sense of community. Joining in the singing and sharing the greeting of peace contribute to her communal experience, but the high point for her is receiving communion, which unites her to Christ and the whole congregation. She knows the truth of Paul's statement: "We, though many, are one body, for we all partake of the one loaf" (1 Corinthians 10:17). Barbara usually leaves Mass with gratitude for the way Christ satisfies her hunger for community and with a renewed commitment to deepen her relationships with her family, friends, and work colleagues.

What is my own deepest spiritual hunger?

90. Do I accept Christ as my king?

In his passion account, John the evangelist highlights the trial of Jesus before Pilate, the Roman governor, concentrating on their initial conversation on the charge that Jesus is a subversive king challenging the authority of Roman rule. In response, Jesus insists that his kingdom is not of this world and that he came into the world "to testify to the truth," adding: "Everyone who belongs to the truth listens to my voice" (John 18: 33-37).

Christ is the faithful witness to the truth. He is the wisdom of the Father. He is the parable of God's truth. He knows human nature and the secrets of the heart. His Kingdom of truth does not originate from this world or belong to it, but it does make an impact on worldly affairs. His life and example reveal the deepest truths about human existence: we are encompassed by God's unconditional love and mercy; we are children of the Father, brothers and sisters to one another; we are temples of the Holy Spirit, who guides us to the truth; we are created in the image of God, who wills eternal happiness for us. Christ is our king who testifies to the most significant truths about ourselves and our relationship to God.

To accept Christ as our king means trying to hear his voice, learn from his example, and appropriate his truths. Some examples: A lawyer who became more aware of how Jesus identified himself with the hungry and thirsty, made a substantial increase in his contributions to the Catholic Campaign for Human Development and vows to do more pro bono work for the poor. A married woman who carried heavy guilt feelings over an abortion she had before she met her husband was moved by Pope Francis to accept God's forgiveness, which lifted her spirits. A waitress, who often feels underappreciated, came to accept Christ's truth that she has inherent worth as a child of God. A retired teacher, who was feeling useless after meaningful years helping students, heard Christ calling him to do volunteer tutoring, which gave him a renewed sense of purpose.

> In what ways does Christ the King actually rule my life, and how could I do a better job of hearing his voice?

91. Am I committed to Christ?

In Matthew's Gospel, Jesus, referring to himself, asks: "Who do people say that the Son of Man is?" (Matthew 6:13-15). Two thousand years later, we can answer that over two billion Christians recognize Jesus as their Savior. Around 1.5 billion Muslims, although denying Jesus is the Son of God, still revere him as a great prophet, a messenger from God, who was conceived miraculously in Mary's womb, performed wondrous miracles, was saved from crucifixion, and was raised by God. In the United States, around three out of four citizens report that they not only believe in Jesus but have sensed his presence. More than two-thirds of U.S. citizens say they have made a personal commitment to Jesus Christ. Many Americans accept Jesus as their personal savior, while others see him as an enlightened sage or a model of vigorous manhood. The current popularity of Jesus is itself a remarkable historical development, especially considering that he died an apparent failure, deserted by his followers, rejected by the religious leaders, and virtually unnoticed by secular history.

All this is important background as we ponder a response to the second, more personal question Jesus poses to each one of us: "But who do you say that I am?" This is a question that demands prayerful reflection and honest self-examination. The Christian claim, verified in the lives of authentic disciples, is that Jesus Christ is the decisive figure in human history, the definitive prophet, the absolute savior, the Son of God. The question put to us by Jesus prompts us to examine this claim and verify its truth by acting on it in our everyday lives. The common element in the responses of authentic disciples is a personal commitment to Christ as the central figure and decisive influence in their lives.

Good Christians express this commitment in various ways. For a young man repenting of his sexual sins, Jesus is the Good Shepherd who goes after strays. For a high school science teacher, Christ is the cosmic Lord who guides and energizes the evolutionary process. A social worker loves the image of Jesus as the liberator of captives. A grandmother often reminds her grandchildren that Jesus has always been her friend and companion on the journey of life. A Jesuit-trained lawyer views Jesus as the exemplary man for others. A history professor puts his faith in the risen Christ, convinced that the resurrection is the only possible explanation for the remarkable enduring influence of Jesus today. A charismatic Catholic is very comfortable talking about Jesus as her personal savior. A factory worker is grateful that Jesus is the great mediator who gives him access to the "Man Upstairs." An idealistic collegian looks to Jesus as the most authentic person who ever lived. An artist imagines Christ as the Icon of the Father, God's greatest artistic work. An avid reader likes to think of Jesus as the main character in the greatest love story ever written, the one authored by God.

Who do you say I am? Answering this crucial question is a lifelong project, an ongoing invitation to prayerful meditation, a continuous opportunity to know ourselves better and to deepen our faith in Christ.

How do I make Christ more important in my life?

92. What role does the resurrection play in my spiritual life?

In Luke's Gospel, the Sadducees, who tended to cooperate with the Romans and confined their religious beliefs to truths found in the scriptures, try to draw Jesus into their theological dispute over the resurrection with the Pharisees, who refused to cooperate with the Roman occupying regime and were open to wider interpretations of scripture, including belief in the resurrection. In order to show that this belief is ridiculous, the Sadducees pose a question to Jesus. A woman was married successively to seven brothers all of whom, faithful to Jewish law, tried to get her pregnant but died before producing an heir. Then the question to Jesus: "In the resurrection, therefore, whose wife will the woman be?"

Taking the side of the Pharisees, Jesus affirms belief in the resurrection. He argues that Moses held a belief in the resurrection when he taught that the God of Abraham, Isaac, and Jacob is "God not of the dead, but of the living; for to him all of them are alive." Death does not break the bonds of love we enjoy with God on this earth. Jesus also teaches that existence in the age to come is quite different from this age. The children of God enjoying the resurrection are no longer subject to death. They are like angels who "neither marry nor are given in marriage." The essential point of the passage is that we live on after death with the loving God in a union that is beyond our words and images (Luke 20: 27-38).

As Christians, we believe in the resurrection of *the body*, as stated in the Apostles Creed, and the resurrection of *the dead*, as we recite in the Nicene Creed. This general belief is fulfilled in Jesus Christ who died for us and was raised to life by God. We share in his risen life now on this earth and will enjoy the fullness of union with Christ in heaven. Belief in the resurrection empowers us to affirm what we hope is true: that life has ultimate meaning; that all of our good efforts are worthwhile; that love is stronger than death; that grace is more powerful than sin; and that the good will finally defeat all the evil forces.

Resurrection faith sustains Christians in various ways. It gives assurance to a mother that her three adult children, who no longer go to Mass but are good compassionate persons, are on a journey leading to heaven and that all of her childrearing efforts have an abiding validity. A husband who lost his wife to cancer at a young age carries on his responsibilities as a single parent, strengthened by the conviction that the love of his life is happy with God and remains a supportive presence to him and their children. A grandfather views the great times spent with his grandchildren as a foretaste of the joys of heaven awaiting him after his death, which draws ever closer.

> How does my faith in the resurrection help me manage the crosses of daily life?

93. What does it mean to me to follow Christ?

In chapter nine of Luke's Gospel, we find some helpful insights on discipleship (Luke 9: 57-62). When a prospective disciple says to Jesus: "I will follow you wherever you go," the Lord replies that he himself has "nowhere to lay his head," suggesting that discipleship is difficult because it does not fit easily into the ordinary ways of the world. Following Jesus puts us on a counter-cultural journey with unexpected challenges and surprising opportunities. For example, a young man, in and out of drug rehab programs, hears Christ's call and stops hanging out with his buddies in the drug scene, while developing a new set of friends who share his Christian values.

In the Gospel, Jesus takes the initiative and invites another individual to follow him. When the man asks permission to go first to bury his father, Jesus says: "Let the dead bury their own dead;

but as for you, go and proclaim the kingdom of God." The call to follow Christ by joining in his mission to spread the reign of God demands immediate action. It cannot be indefinitely delayed pending other events, even the death of a loved one. Christian discipleship has an urgency about it; now is the moment of decision; this is the hour for action on behalf of the kingdom. For example, a couple who passively endured a troubled marriage for years heard this message and immediately began marriage counseling, which has enriched their marriage.

Still another man in the Gospel tells Jesus he wants to follow him but asks for the opportunity to say farewell to his family. Jesus responds: "No one who puts a hand to the plow and looks back is fit for the kingdom of God." Following Christ is the most important thing life, the highest priority. It requires total dedication that is not concerned with keeping options open or worried about other missed opportunities. Effective Christian disciples keep their hand to the plough, working wholeheartedly for the cause of God in the world. For example, a single woman totally devoted to advancing her career was struck by a homily on this passage that emphasized keeping our priorities straight. After a lot of prayerful reflection leading to a firm decision, she began devoting more time and energy to her family and friends as well as to her parish social justice program. She felt more fulfilled and has no regrets about her new set of priorities.

> How could I deepen and expand my commitment to follow Christ?

94. Where can I find mercy and forgiveness?

The evangelist Matthew reports the call of Matthew, a tax collector, who immediately follows Jesus (Matthew 9: 9-13). The next thing we know, Jesus is dining at Matthew's house with a lot of other disreputable people. Pharisees see this and ask the disciples of Jesus why their teacher eats with sinners. Overhearing this, Jesus responds: "Those who are well have no need of a physician, but those who are sick go and learn what this means, 'I desire mercy, not sacrifice.' For I have come to call not the righteous but sinners."

The scripture scholars provide helpful background on the Gospel. Matthew the tax collector is not Matthew the evangelist who wrote the Gospel. Tax collectors were despised by their fellow Jews because they collaborated with the oppressive Roman regime and were often guilty of extorting extra taxes for their own benefit. By dining with people like them, Jesus broke the law and rendered himself ritually impure, while by their strict observance of the Jewish law, the Pharisees avoided being coopted by Roman pagan culture. The pronouncements of Jesus at the end of the passage, however, highlight God's special care for sinners, the priority of mercy over ritual sacrifice, and his own mission to those estranged from God in any way, which includes all of us.

We can imagine contemporary positive responses to this Gospel message. A man long estranged from his brother now prays at every Mass for the gift of reconciliation and for guidance on how to reach out to him. A woman who is very disappointed that over the years she has made little progress in becoming more tolerant of others decides to keep trying, despite her failures. Recognizing that he has been coopted into a consumerist culture, a respected judge determines to simplify his life and do more pro bono work for the poor. A Catholic woman who never felt worthy or adequate to get involved in her parish, answers Christ's call and now is very active serving as a lector and member of the liturgy committee.

What concrete step could I take to respond better to Christ, who came to call sinners?

95. Am I ready to take up the cross to follow Christ?

In Mark's version of the same story in Matthew, Jesus seems to be checking the response to his healing and preaching ministry by asking his disciples: "Who do people say that I am?" (Mark 8:27-35). Evidently, many think he is one of the prophets returned to life, perhaps John the Baptist or Elijah. Then Jesus turns to his disciples, asking them a more personal, engaging question: "But who do you say that I am?" Responding out of his Jewish religious tradition, Peter replies "You are the Messiah," indicating that he saw Jesus as the anointed one of God. Jesus uses the opportunity to teach his disciples that he must suffer rejection and be killed by the religious leaders. Peter does not want to hear this, earning a strong rebuke from Jesus, who then summons the crowd to instruct them in the harsh truth that they must take up the cross to follow him.

This passage invites us to engage the question of the identity of Jesus in an honest, personal way. Who is Christ for me? To identify ourselves as one of the 2.2 billion Christians in the world today means that in one way or another we see Christ as central to our lives and as exercising decisive influence on how we live. In answering that question, Mark warns us against easy answers that effectively deny that Christ was a suffering servant: for example, seeing him as a Santa Claus figure who favors faithful believers with a comfortable, prosperous life or as a divine person who was spared the hard lot of a fully human existence.

Let us imagine individual Christians testifying to the centrality of Christ in their lives in their own unique ways. "Jesus who suffered and died to save us helps me deal with my many health problems." "The Teacher who had no place to lay his head gives me motivation to keep looking for a job." "Christ who forgave his executioners enabled me to forgive my emotionally abusive father." "Jesus who went about doing good in a troubled world is my main model for keeping high moral standards in the competitive world of business." "Christ who identified with the hungry and thirsty encourages me to maintain my commitment to serve the poor." "Jesus who called his disciples friends keeps me going on a bad day." "Christ who walked with his disciples assures me that the crosses I encounter can lead to a richer life."

> How does Christ help me deal with the sufferings of life?

96. How do I relate to Christ the Liberator?

Luke tells us that Jesus, who was preaching throughout Galilee, returned to his home town of Nazareth, and went to the synagogue on the Sabbath as was his custom. During the service, he stood up and read a passage (Isaiah 11: 1-2) about a prophet anointed by the Lord who is to proclaim glad tidings to the poor, liberty to captives, and freedom to the oppressed. Jesus then sat down and with all eyes toward him, declared, "Today this scripture has been fulfilled in your hearing" (Luke 4:21).

With this remarkable declaration, Jesus identified himself as the Messiah and set out the general theme of his liberating ministry. He proved to be an effective liberator, in part because he himself was open to the Spirit, free of compulsions, willing to respond to the call of his Father. His liberating power took various forms: exorcising individuals held captive by demonic forces; instructing those confined by their own ignorance; curing people burdened by illness; encouraging persons limited by their fears; and forgiving those imprisoned in their sinfulness.

As the Christian community today reflects on Christ the liberator of captives, we can envision various individual responses: A social activist finds encouragement to keep working for prison reform. A grandmother trapped in a serious drinking problem joins Alcoholic Anonymous. A young man near the end of his six-month jail sentence for drug possession makes a firm decision to completely avoid the drug scene when he gets out. A husband burdened by temptations to adultery follows the advice of a counselor to satisfy his strong desires within his marriage. A woman addicted to gossip does a face-to-face confession to get guidance on freeing herself from this unattractive habit. A grandfather very limited by a grade-school understanding of his faith, reads his collegiate granddaughter's theology textbook so he can have a serious conversation with her.

> What can I learn by reflecting on Christ the liberator of captives, and how can I respond better to his liberating message?

97. Where can I find wisdom for life?

John tells us that the Jews were murmuring about Jesus because he said he came "down from heaven" while they know him as the son of Joseph. Jesus responds with the striking claim that he comes from the Father, whom he alone has seen. He goes on to identify himself as "the living bread that comes down from heaven" adding that "whoever eats of this bread will live forever" (John 6: 41-51).

The scripture scholars tell us that this section of the long Bread of Life discourse in the sixth chapter of John's Gospel reflects the Old Testament teaching on divine wisdom as our food or bread. In this passage, we encounter Jesus as the One who teaches divine wisdom, the Son who knows the secrets of the Father, the Word who reveals the life-giving truths of God. He is himself the wisdom of the Father, the parable of God, the embodiment of divine truth. By his example and teaching, he guides to us to a richer life on earth and to the fullness of life in heaven. He is the living bread that enlightens our mind and illumines the path to spiritual growth.

A composite story highlights the point. Junia, a woman in her early fifties, lived for over a decade with extreme anger at her older brother who cheated her out of her fair share of the family inheritance when their father died. Obsessed with the cruel injustices of her brother's shady maneuvers, she held tight to vengeful feelings that led to depression, sleepless nights, and unwarranted angry outbursts directed at her family and friends.

One Sunday, Junia heard a homily on forgiveness that presented Jesus as the great reconciler who taught forgiveness by example (forgiving his executioners) and by word (the Lord's Prayer). The preacher went on to say that harboring angry thoughts toward others poisons our hearts and can cause emotional problems. The only antidote to this poison is forgiveness, which does not demand forgetting injustice but does involve viewing offenders as more than their hurtful deeds and allowing them to begin again with us. Reflecting on the homily, Junia simply decided to forgive her brother and succeeded in taking away his power to continue to hurt her. She immediately began to feel better, more peaceful and less agitated. Junia now knows, not theoretically but experientially, that Christ is indeed the living bread, the Wisdom of the Father, who reveals to us the deepest truths about human existence and teaches us how to live wisely and fruitfully.

> What have I learned from Christ that helps me live wisely, and how could I appropriate more of his infinite wisdom?

98. How can I be more open to Christ's forgiveness?

In John's Gospel, Jesus was teaching in the outer court of the Temple when the scribes and Pharisees presented a woman caught in the act of adultery and asked Jesus whether she should be stoned to death as commanded by Moses. It was a clever trap: if Jesus says yes, he goes against his teaching on compassionate forgiveness and puts himself in conflict with the Romans who reserved capital punishment to themselves; if he says no, he alienates the Jews who interpreted the Mosaic law strictly. Avoiding the trap, Jesus wrote on the ground and said: "Let anyone among you who is without sin be the first to throw a stone at her." After he wrote on the ground a second time, her accusers went away one by one beginning with the elders. Left alone with her, Jesus noted that no one was there to condemn her, and declared: "Neither do I condemn you. Go your way, and from now on do not sin again" (John 8: 1-11).

Jesus cleverly avoided the trap set for him by the religious leaders, shaming them and gaining respect for himself. In the process, he reinforced his consistent teaching on mercy, forgiveness, and compassion. Jesus is the face of God's mercy. His example and teaching proclaim the good news that we are not imprisoned in our past sins, mistakes, and failures. With God's help there are fresh starts, new beginnings, second chances, and clean slates. Sin tends to confine, constrict, and imprison, while grace liberates, opens new possibilities, and restores hope. Jesus had mercy on a woman separated from her paramour, exposed to public shame, victimized by a patriarchal system, used with evil intent, and threatened by death—thus offering her the opportunity to cast off all these burdens and begin anew.

The Christian claim is that Christ can do the same for us today, liberating us from our sins and opening up a better future for us. Some people know this to be true from personal experience. An elderly woman celebrating the Sacrament of Reconciliation mentioned, as she always does, her major fault of being judgmental. The priest suggested as a penance that she pay someone an honest complement each day for a month. Diligent in doing the penance, she found herself having surprisingly fewer judgmental thoughts about her relatives and friends and seeing them in a much more positive light. A young man with a long-standing masturbation problem started praying to the Lord each night for the gift of greater sexual maturity, which seemed to reduce the intensity and frequency of his temptations.

> Have I experienced forgiveness in my life, and has it been liberating?

99. Do I accept Jesus as Lord of the Sabbath?

Mark recounts two stories of conflict between the Pharisees and Jesus over Sabbath observance (Mark 2: 23-3: 6). In the first, the opponents of Jesus chide him because his disciples pick grain while passing through a field and thus, in their interpretation, break the law by working on the Sabbath. Jesus responds by reminding them that King David fed his hungry companions with the bread of offering that only the priest could lawfully eat.

In the second story, Jesus cures a man with a withered hand in the synagogue, once again incurring the wrath of the Pharisees, who immediately conspired with the Herodians to kill him. For his part, Jesus was angry and grieved at their hardness of heart. For him the issue was clear: "The sabbath was made for humankind, and not humankind for the sabbath." He said this claiming supreme authority for himself, "so the Son of Man is lord even of the sabbath."

The Gospel reminds us of important truths about Jesus. He is the definitive prophet; the wisdom of the Father; the Divine Physician who heals body and soul; the Son of Man who judges all people; the community builder; the liberator of captives; and the Lord of the Sabbath. He teaches us that people are more important than laws; that love of neighbor, which always includes love of God, is the most important law; that attending to individuals in need may supersede customary traditions and rules; that a discernment process may produce a moral obligation not covered by universal norms.

Many Christians today recognize the limitations of legalistic approaches to moral decision-making. Let us imagine the personal testimony of Rosie, an older cradle Catholic: "I have been a strict Catholic all my life, committed to following the laws of God and of the Church. Recently, my husband got sick on Sunday morning right before we were going to Mass together as we do every weekend. I stayed home all day attending to him and never got to Mass. It is interesting to me that I felt no guilt about missing Mass and have no doubt I did the right thing. I remember about thirty years ago a similar situation when my daughter was ill and I missed Sunday Mass. At that time, I did have guilt feelings and felt a need to go to Confession before receiving Communion again. I feel I have grown spiritually and am now more in tune with Christ who is Lord of the Sabbath."

Let us envision another personal witness, Karl. "A few years ago, a black family was trying to move into our all white suburban gated community. Our neighbors wanted us to support an effort, based on some legal technicality, to keep then out, but my wife and I refused to join in on the grounds that discrimination is morally wrong and our faith demands that we love and respect all people. Our neighbors were upset with us, but we felt we did the right thing. When the black family actually moved in, we prayed privately for them and felt called by God to reach out to them and try to make them feel welcome, which we did. In the process we learned that people in need are not only more important than discriminatory laws but also that they deserve special care and respect."

> What can I do to be more faithful to Christ,
> the Lord of the Sabbath?

100. How can I share more deeply in the life of Christ?

In John's Gospel, Jesus speaks of his mission: "I came that they may have life, and have it abundantly" (John 10: 1-10). Christ has come not to restrict our freedom or limit our happiness but to help us develop our potential, find a fulfilling purpose, and become a more effective force for good. This is good news that touches our deepest longings: a recent college graduate is looking for a job that is personally fulfilling; a young woman wants a life partner who will help her grow spiritually; a mother of two youngsters joins a book club, hoping for intellectual stimulation; a retired consultant wants to do volunteer work that will give him a sense of purpose. We all know something of the quest for a more abundant life.

Jesus, who came to give us a more abundant life, was himself the most mature, fulfilled, energetic, alive person who ever lived. Christ reveals to us the dynamics and shape of the abundant human life. John's Gospel presents Jesus as the good shepherd who knows us by name, guides us on the path, and provides the gate for entering the pasture of salvation. We find the more abundant life by listening to Christ and following him.

As the first letter of Peter reminds us, Christ suffered for us, leaving an example for us to follow in his footsteps. His suffering was the byproduct of his life of self-sacrificing love. His death led to the abundant life of the risen Lord. Through his death and resurrection, he became life-giving spirit for us. As the crucified and risen Lord, he is himself the gate to the more abundant life.

We do not earn this abundant life, but we receive it as a gift. We find ourselves living more fully when we follow Christ's example of self-sacrificing love. Egocentricity restricts life; love opens our hearts to the gift of abundant life.

We can imagine witnesses to this truth. A secretary: "After I put aside my pride and reconciled with a colleague at the office, my work has been more fulfilling." A wife: "When I stopped nagging my husband so much and paid him more honest compliments, our marriage became more life-giving for both of us." A volunteer: "Since I started serving as a Big Brother to an inner-city teenager, I have felt alive in a new way with a greater sense of purpose." Christ the shepherd does indeed call each one of us by name, while promising the gift of abundant life to those who follow his example of self-sacrificing love.

> What specific step could I take to be more receptive to Christ's gift of abundant life?

101. Do I recognize the voice of the Good Shepherd?

In John's Gospel, Jesus presents himself as the Good Shepherd who has a close, intimate relationship with his sheep and lays down his life for them (John 10: 11-18). The Good Shepherd, crucified and risen, knows the joys and sorrows of the human condition and calls each one of us by name. He shares his Spirit with us, calling all people into a communion of love where God reigns so that there will be one flock, one shepherd.

The Church is the sign and instrument of the reign of God, that communion of loving intimacy inaugurated and sustained by the Good Shepherd. As members of that Church, we celebrate our intimate relationship with Christ and accept our responsibility to share that gift with others. We who recognize the voice of the Shepherd must call others by name, recognizing them as unique individuals with distinctive gifts and specific needs.

We celebrate those who serve others with loving respect: the father who knows how to meet the very different needs of each of his four children; the dentist who does pro bono work for the poor and tries to learn something from each person she serves;

the doctor who treats individual patients and not generic diseases; the receptionist for a large corporation who remembers the names of clients and greets them warmly; the teacher who spends extra time helping slower students; and the pastor who recognizes the gifts of individual parishioners and empowers them to use their talents to build up the Body of Christ.

> Do I appreciate my intimate relationship with the Good Shepherd, and how can I share that blessing with others?

102. How can I stay alive spiritually?

"I am the vine, you are the branches," says Jesus in John's Gospel, adding that if we remain in him we will "bear much fruit" (John 15: 1-8). Through his death and resurrection Christ has become for us the life-giving Spirit. The crucified and risen Lord is the always available source of our nourishment and energy. Our challenge is to develop a relationship with Christ and stay in touch with him so that we can grow spiritually and share in his mission to spread the reign of God in the world.

In the Gospel, Jesus warns that we will wither and die spiritually if separated from him. Examples come to mind: an energetic Catholic peace activist stops going to Mass entirely and finds that he is gradually losing motivation for the cause; a mother of two teenagers drops her longstanding habit of praying for her children in the morning and discovers that she has started running out of energy to deal with them throughout the day.

On the other hand, we can imagine individuals who bear fruit by staying in touch with Christ in various ways. A municipal judge maintains a Christ-like respect for individual defendants, helping some to get on a more productive path. A social worker grows spiritually and does her job more effectively by seeing Christ in her clients. A vowed sister who prays every day to Christ for the grace to be more tolerant and less judgmental becomes a force for good in her community, helping to create a more harmonious spirit.

> How can I give better witness in my daily work to my relationship to Christ the Vine?

103. What does it mean to participate in the Paschal Mystery?

"Very truly, I tell you, unless a grain of wheat falls into the earth and dies, it remains just a single grain; but if it dies, it bears much fruit" (John 12: 24). The Gospel links this fundamental teaching of Jesus to his own death, (lifted up from the earth on the cross) and his resurrection. Reflecting on his pending death, Jesus is "troubled," but accepts the hour of his death as an essential element in the divine plan for saving the world and drawing everyone to himself.

We call the fruitful dynamic between the death and the risen life of Christ the "Paschal Mystery." Jesus calls his disciples to share in his Paschal sacrifice by dying to self in order to gain eternal life. The daily deaths involved in self-sacrificing love are fruitful, leading to a deeper participation in the glorified life of the risen Christ. The daily deaths prompted by faithful discipleship prepare us for that decisive hour when we can make definitive and irreversible our option for God. The Gospel claim is that death leads to life; that self-sacrificing love issues in a more fulfilled existence; that sharing in the death of Christ enables us to share in his resurrection.

We find inspiration in the Christians who testify to the truth of this claim. A married man reports that his marriage became more fulfilling when he let go of his self-centered expectations and became more attentive to the needs of his wife. A successful advertising consultant became a more satisfied and balanced person when she stopped making an idol out of her job. A collegian with limited intellectual capabilities became more peaceful and energetic when he abandoned his unrealistic dream of becoming a doctor. A senior citizen enjoying his life of leisure after retirement got a new lease on life after he volunteered some of his time helping inner city kids. A mother eventually found greater inner peace when she lets go of her anger at God for the suicide death of her collegiate son.

> Have I had any experiences that verify the paschal
> teaching of Jesus? What did they teach me?

Chapter Five

Ecclesiology (forming the People of God)

104. Do I recognize Christ in the breaking of the Bread?

Luke begins one of his appearance stories with Cleopas and his unnamed companion telling the other disciples how they had met Jesus on the road to Emmaus and recognized him in the breaking of the bread. Then the risen Christ appears to the disciples, offers them a greeting of peace, shows them his wounds, eats in front of them, and enjoins them to serve as witnesses of these things (Luke 24: 35-48).

This appearance story reminds us of the table fellowship that was an important part of the ministry of Jesus: sharing meals with his disciples; eating in the homes of opponents and sinners; and especially the Last Supper, when he shared bread and wine with his disciples, his body and blood offered for the salvation of the world. It also directs our attention to our celebrations of the Eucharist, when we have encountered Christ present in the assembly, in the proclamation of the scriptural word, and in the sacred meal of bread and wine.

As did Cleopas, we can bear witness to recognizing Christ in "the breaking of the bread." A father confides to his son that going to Mass every Sunday has made him a better husband. A devout Catholic wife tells her Protestant husband how much it means to her that he goes to church with her on Saturday afternoon. A young girl tells her friend how special her First Communion was. A grandfather tries to be especially attentive to his grandchildren on those occasions when they go to Mass with him. A woman invites her non-practicing sister to join her at Mass in her parish where the community is welcoming, the music upbeat, and the homily is usually relevant. A retired man who generally prefers quick Masses tells his friends how moved he was by the long Easter Vigil service.

> Are there times when we have recognized Christ in the breaking of the bread, and how might we give witness to these encounters?

105. How can Lent help me overcome my temptations?

Mark's version of the temptations of Jesus is brief but filled with symbolic meaning (Mark 1: 12-15). The Spirit that guided Israel's judges, kings, and prophets; that overshadowed Mary; and descended on Jesus in his baptism; drives him into the wilderness, a dangerous place with wild beasts where he will be tested—as was Israel during its forty years wandering in the desert. Reminiscent of the forty-day fasts of Moses and Elijah, Jesus fasts for forty days in preparation for his encounter with Satan, the personification of evil, who roams the world tempting people to turn away from God. Aided by the ministry of angels, Jesus survives the ordeal and begins proclaiming the gospel of God in Galilee.

As we struggle with our own temptations, this reading from Mark offers encouragement and guidance. Temptations are built into human existence. Even Jesus, who was like us in all things but sin, knew temptations in his life. We all know the lure of common temptations: to flee from God, to refuse to accept our limitations as creatures, to escape from reality, to seek total control of our lives, to choose estrangement over communion, to opt for expediency over principle, to make idols out of finite realities.

In our encounters with Satan, we can count on the assistance of the Holy Spirit, the Advocate who lives within us. The Spirit that drove Jesus into the desert is the same Spirit that gives us wisdom and strength to resist temptations. The gift of wisdom enables us to name accurately the demons that attack us and to identify the disciplines needed to transform the temptation into positive energy on behalf of God's reign.

Lent is a good time to identify one of our main temptations and choose an appropriate penance to do throughout the season. A woman who is periodically tempted to gossip about her affluent neighbor could try to say at least one kind thing about her each week of Lent. A man worried about falling back into his old drinking habits could attend more AA meetings. A busy executive who tends toward workaholism could plan on doing more leisure activities with his family. A mother tempted to think she is too busy to pray could take as her Lenten penance at least five minutes of prayer each day. A young man tempted to visit porn sites on his computer could try to divert his attention by a program of vigorous daily exercise. A woman who struggles with overeating could use Lent to develop healthy eating habits.

> What is my most troublesome temptation and what Lenten penance would help me overcome it?

106. How can I grow spiritually during Advent?

Mark preserves for each one of us an urgent message from Jesus: "Beware, keep alert" for we don't know when the time will come (Mark 13: 33-37). We all know something of the temptation to sleepwalk through life: missing opportunities to grow spiritually, to help others, to serve the common good. We can be so busy and self-absorbed that promptings of the Spirit go unnoticed.

The Gospel serves as a wakeup call from Christ himself. The reign of God is near, at the doorstep, on the edge of our consciousness. We are immersed in a divine milieu, a graced world, a Spirit-filled environment. All things, including the most mundane, ordinary, routine activities of life are potentially revelatory, capable of bearing a word from the Lord. It is possible to discern the presence of the Holy Spirit in very diverse places and situations: in the kitchen and the bedroom; in work and leisure; in the extraordinary and the ordinary; in the familiar and the strange; in victory and defeat. Nothing that is truly human is off limits to the Spirit.

During the season of Advent, Christ is calls us to be more mindful of the diverse opportunities to encounter the Spirit and respond to the revelatory moments. Ideally, we would develop habits of mindfulness during our preparation for Christmas that would make us more attentive to the presence of the Spirit throughout the year. The spiritual masters provide traditional wisdom for mining the richness of the season: participate more attentively in the Advent liturgies; read scripture, open to a personal message; spend time in spiritual reading that touches the heart; practice a meditation technique that calms the mind and sharpens awareness; say brief prayers throughout the day; do an examination of conscience each night before going to sleep.

Practically, it is very difficult during the hectic month of December to cultivate mindfulness, but not impossible as the following examples suggest. A mother of two small children gets more out of Sunday Mass by looking over the scripture readings the night before. An electrician, who learned the Ignatian method of meditation on a retreat, keeps himself focused by meditating twice a week, imagining himself a witness to various miracles of Jesus. A family cultivates the virtue of gratitude by spending a few minutes before dinner giving each person an opportunity to say a prayer of thanks for a specific blessing received that day. During Advent, a married couple chooses a spiritual book to read and discuss together once a week, often leading to a greater appreciation of each other. A busy executive, who examines her conscience each night for missed opportunities to meet the needs of colleagues and friends, finds that this practice makes her more present to others.

> What could I do during Advent to become more watchful and alert?

107. What can I learn from Luke's account of the temptations of Christ?

Luke reports the temptations of Jesus in the desert to turn stones into bread, to gain worldly power by worshipping the devil, and to put God to the test by jumping from the top of the Jerusalem Temple. These temptations are all subtle inducements for Jesus to deny his human limitations and his total dependence on God. In each case, Jesus rejects the temptation, citing a text from Deuteronomy that highlights God's sovereignty. Luke concludes the passage: "When the devil had finished every test, he departed from him until an opportune time" suggesting that Jesus had to deal with temptations throughout his life as do we (Luke 4: 1-13).

Considering the temptations of Jesus as common to all of us, we can imagine individuals who have followed the good example of the Lord in managing them. Through most of his life, Karl was a hard driving, success-oriented person who placed a higher priority on providing an affluent lifestyle for his family then on cultivating his own spiritual life. One year reflecting on this Gospel, he was struck with the response of Jesus to the devil: "One does not live on bread alone." Suddenly he saw himself not only as a breadwinner but as a man called to develop his spiritual life by following the will of God, putting on the mind of Christ, and listening to the prompting of the Holy Spirit. Recognizing the temptation to remain in the grasp of his material mindset, he undertook a serious spiritual regimen of daily meditation, preparation for Sunday Mass, and guided reading of the Bible, which over time transformed his priorities in life.

Influenced by the common slogan "you can have it all," Jeanne drove herself to exhaustion, striving to be the best mother possible, putting in extra time furthering her promising career, and making a name for herself through community service. Reflecting on the Gospel, she realized she had made an idol out of "having it all" and that she would make better decisions about her life if she concentrated on the words of Jesus "You shall worship the Lord your God and him alone shall you serve."

Bob, a bachelor in his early thirties, lives on the edge, drinking too much, experimenting with drugs, and engaging in unprotected sex. His girlfriend, Amy, got him to go to Mass, where he heard the words of Jesus, "You shall not put the Lord your God, to the test," which spoke to his heart. With a shock of recognition, he knew he was guilty of testing God and that he had to turn his life around.

> Which of the temptations of Christ speak to my heart, and how can I become a more faithful disciple?

108. Do I hear the call to holiness?

In Luke's Gospel, an experienced but frustrated fisherman reluctantly takes the advice of a carpenter from Nazareth and has an amazing catch that fills his boat and the boat of his partners as well. When the fisherman, Simon (later Peter) by name, saw this, he fell at the feet of Jesus. The carpenter- turned-itinerate-preacher told him, "Go away from me, Lord, for I am a sinful man!" Jesus tells Simon not to be afraid "from now on you will be catching people." When Simon and his business partners, James and John, the sons of Zebedee, got their boats ashore, they left their livelihood and their families and followed Jesus (Luke 5: 1-11).

Jesus attracted many other disciples by the power of his personality, his teaching, and his wondrous deeds. Some like Peter, left everything to follow him, but many others--Mary, Martha and Lazarus, for example—stayed at home and kept their jobs, putting the example and teaching of Jesus into practice in their daily lives. Throughout history, there has been a tendency to exalt the disciples who renounce ordinary life in the world while relegating the stay-at-home disciples to a secondary status. In effect, this mostly meant restricting the word "vocation" and the call to holiness to priests, nuns, and brothers. The Second Vatican Council (1962-1965) reversed this trend by teaching that all the baptized have a vocation, all are responsible for building up the Body of Christ and spreading the reign of God in the world, and all are called to holiness. There are no second-class members of the Church.

Many Catholics have grown spiritually and became more effective disciples by appropriating the Vatican II teaching on the common vocation to holiness. Abraham, a cradle Catholic, who for a good part of his adult life was content to let the pastor run the parish, took some classes on Vatican II and is now very active in his parish, serving on the finance council and the liturgy committee. Sarah, a dedicated stay-at-home mother of three who sometimes felt inadequate because she did not have a paying job outside the home, became far more comfortable with her chosen role when she thought of it as a true vocation which is her path to holiness. Isaac, a talented marketing grad student who worried that pursuing a career in the business world was selling out to the consumerist culture, heard a homily on the spirituality of work that convinced him he could, in good conscience, take a job with a marketing firm and use it as a way of living his faith and contributing to the common good. Stephanie, a single mother, who felt sort of useless after her two children left home and started their own families, came to see that she had a second vocation as a grandmother who could still do a lot of good.

> What does the universal call to holiness mean to me, and how can I respond more wholeheartedly?

109. How can I gain a greater appreciation of the Scriptures?

In Luke's Gospel, the risen Christ opens the minds of his disciples so they can understand the scriptures and can be witnesses to his death and resurrection, proclaiming repentance and forgiveness of sins in his name to all nations. After that, Jesus led his disciples to Bethany where he blessed them and was carried up into heaven (Luke 24: 45-53).

As Christians today, we believe that Christ can help us understand the scriptures so we can give testimony to the liberating power of his death and resurrection. The Bible is the normative witness to God's saving activity in the world. The biblical story of salvation culminates in the life, death, and resurrection of Jesus Christ: the Son of God, the absolute savior, and the definitive prophet.

Since the Second Vatican Council in the 1960s, Catholics have gained a greater appreciation of the scriptures. They hear a good portion of the Bible proclaimed at Sunday liturgies over a three-year cycle. Many Catholics are involved in small faith sharing groups based on the liturgical readings. Catholics now read the Bible privately in search of spiritual nourishment and wisdom. For example, Alice, a grandmother who was discouraged from reading the bible in her youth because of the dangers of private interpretation now spends about half an hour a day doing the traditional spiritual exercise known as "lectio divina." She begins with a prayer asking God for a receptive heart, then slowly reads a passage from one of the Gospels, pausing to reflect when she senses a thought or image relevant for her life. After she has exhausted that point, she returns to a slow reading of the Gospel text, prepared to pause again when something strikes her. At the end of her encounter with Christ in the scriptures, Alice says a prayer of gratitude for any insight and inspiration she has received.

The passage from Luke also reminds us of our obligation to give witness to the repentance and forgiveness unleashed by the death and resurrection of Christ. Jacob an electrician who grew up in a white family with deep prejudices against black Americans, carried racist attitudes into his adult life. He was part of a movement to keep blacks out of his neighborhood, repeated racial stereotypes in his conversations, and avoided contact with black coworkers. One year, at the Good Friday service in his parish, it suddenly and forcefully struck him that Christ died not just for him but for all people, including African Americans. In a flash of insight, Jacob knew he had to do a complete turnaround, overcoming his prejudice and making up for his overt discrimination. He began this process by engaging each of his three adult children in serious one-to-one conversations: confessing his own sins of racism; expressing his fears that he had passed on to his children a terrible prejudice; explaining his new more open attitude to people of color; and exhorting them to adopt a genuinely Christ-like attitude toward people who are different. He was not sure how effective these conversations were, but he was glad that he made an initial effort, realizing that he had much more to do.

How could I develop a spirituality more solidly grounded in the scriptures and better prepare myself to give witness to the power of Christ's death and resurrection?

110. What can I learn from the Transfiguration?

In Luke's version of the Transfiguration, Jesus takes Peter, James, and John up the mountain to pray. While they fall asleep, Jesus becomes so deep in prayer that his face changes in appearance and his clothing becomes dazzling white. Then he is conversing with Moses and Elijah about his own exodus—his death and resurrection in Jerusalem. Peter and his companions wake up and see Jesus in his glory with the two prophets. Bewildered, Peter starts talking about building three tents, when a cloud casts a shadow over them and they hear a voice, "This is my Son, my Chosen; listen to him!" (Luke 9: 28-36).

Luke's version reminds us that Jesus is God's beloved Son, a man of prayer, the full revelation of God's glory, the new Moses, and the definitive prophet fulfilling the role of Elijah. The passion and death of Jesus will lead to his glorious resurrection. We reflect on the Transfiguration as people called to take up our cross each day. We know something of depressing loneliness, nagging ailments, failed ideals, troubled relationships, tedious labor, disturbing emotions, and confused thoughts. The transfigured Lord encourages us to bear our unavoidable crosses gracefully, confident that they lead to a share in Christ's glory.

Our reflection on the Gospel also reminds us of our own transfiguration experiences, when God's ever-present glory breaks through in our own lives: producing unmerited gifts, surprising strength, renewed idealism, fresh insights, reconnected relationships, meaningful work, and spiritual growth. When we walk at times in the dark valley of everyday life, we do well to remember those mountaintop moments when Gods' glory was more clearly manifest. A devoted wife is kind and patient with her husband suffering from severe dementia, periodically thanking God for the good years they shared. A religious sister who seldom feels any consolation in her daily prayers, perseveres anyway, strengthened by the faith conviction that her cross brings her closer to Christ. A father grieving the repeated drug relapses of his teenage son remains supportive, hoping that the fundamental goodness he has seen in him will prevail.

> What does the Transfiguration mean to me, and how does it affect my everyday life?

111. What scene in Luke's Passion narrative most inspires me?

The Passion according to Luke, a narrative with great dramatic power, presents Jesus as a non-violent innocent victim, who continues to minister to others with remarkable compassion despite his own intense suffering (Luke 22: 14 – 23:56). At their farewell supper, for example, Jesus prays for his disciples that they would have strength to recover from their failures. Describing the arrest of Jesus, only Luke tells us that Jesus healed the right ear of the servant of the high priest severed by one of his disciples. After Peter denied Jesus three times, Jesus looked at Peter with a glance that was, we can imagine, more compassionate then disapproving. On his way to Calvary, Jesus comforted the Daughters of Jerusalem who were lamenting his fate. He prayed for his executioners: "Father, forgive them; for they do not know what they are doing." To the repentant criminal executed with him, Jesus said: "Truly I tell you, today you will be with me in Paradise." Throughout his whole public life and to the very end, Jesus was indeed the compassionate healer.

We can imagine hearers of Luke's passion account being touched by particular scenes. An elderly man says: "I like to think that Christ has been praying for me as he did for the disciples that I could bounce back from my failures." A woman dealing with breast cancer prays: "Lord you healed the servant's ear, please grant me the gift of restored health." A young adult trying once again to escape the drug scene thinks: "If the Lord gave Peter another chance maybe there is hope for me." A single mother worn out from holding a job and raising two kids prays: "Lord I need the kind of comfort you offered to the Daughters of Jerusalem." A husband who ruined his marriage by repeated infidelities, reflects on Jesus forgiving his executioners and thinks to himself: "Maybe there is still a chance for me to make amends, to get my life together, and to be forgiven." A retired philosophy professor, who is still struggling with doubts of faith as he faces death, reflects long and hard on the words of Jesus to the repentant thief and finds a glimmer of hope for his own salvation.

> What specific step could I take today to share in Christ's Passion?

112. How can I make Easter Mass more spiritually enriching?

In John's Gospel, Mary of Magdala discovers the tomb of Jesus is empty and reports this to Peter and the other disciple, the "one whom Jesus loved." They run to the tomb; the other disciple gets there first but waits for Peter to enter before him. Peter sees the burial cloths but no body. Then the other disciple enters, observes the same scene, and he believes (John 20: 1-9). In John's Gospel, the other disciple, who is never named, believed that God raised the crucified Lord to life, supported by the meaning of the empty tomb. Other disciples believed because the risen Christ appeared to them directly, as happened with Thomas, Peter, and the other disciples.

We bring to the joyful celebration of Easter, the most important liturgical celebration of the year, our deepest hopes: that our life has ultimate meaning; that death does not have the final word; that our life journey has a fulfilling destination; that nothing of our good efforts are finally wasted; that love is stronger than death; that our deceased loved ones enjoy eternal happiness, and that one day we will join them. Easter proclaims that we can dare to believe that these deep hopes will ultimately be fulfilled. Contemplating the faith of the "Beloved Disciple" strengthens our conviction that Christ has triumphed over death and shares his risen life with us. This is the core of the Gospel, the fundamental Christian truth, the essence of the good news, the conviction that governs the whole New Testament. Our belief in the Paschal Mystery, which encompasses the death and victorious resurrection of Christ, is strengthened by a fruitful dialogue between our deepest hopes and the testimony of the Gospel.

Our liturgical celebration of Easter invites us to reflect on all the small paschal triumphs that have brought joy to our lives and have reinforced our faith that God did indeed raise the crucified Lord to life. Some examples of paschal victories triggered by Lenten penances: a middle-aged woman battling a weight problem spent Lent developing better eating habits and by Easter was enjoying a new sense of wellbeing and vitality; a husband worked hard to listen better to his wife and came to see her as a more interesting and attractive partner; a man cut down on his drinking in social situations and found himself enjoying them more; a grad student who studied harder during the semester discovers a new sense of self-confidence when taking exams; a parishioner who set aside time to reflect on the readings before Mass was amazed at the way the Liturgy of the Word nourished his spiritual life; a suburban couple who dedicated themselves to helping revitalize an inner city neighborhood found a new sense of purpose in life.

Can I recall the small paschal victories in my own life that reinforce my faith in the resurrection of Christ?

113. Do I experience Christ's presence at Mass?

In Mark's account of the institution of the Eucharist at the Last Supper, Jesus gathered his disciples in a spacious upper room to celebrate the Jewish Passover. During the meal, He took bread, said the blessing, broke it, and gave it to his disciples saying "Take; this is my body." Then he shared a cup of wine with them, saying "This is my blood of the covenant, which is poured out for many" (Mark 14: 22-25).

Today we continue to gather to share the sacred meal of bread and wine, the body and blood of Christ given as our food and drink. As Vatican II taught, Christ is present in the worshipping assembly, in the proclamation of the Scriptures, and in the consecrated bread and wine shared by the community. Celebrating the Eucharist is a prime way for Christians to satisfy the hungers of the heart: for meaning and purpose in life; for genuine community that sustains and guides us; for energy and strength that helps us manage the demands of daily life; for a solid hope that the longings of our heart will be ultimately fulfilled in the Eternal Banquet. The liturgy is indeed the font of the Christian life, the central act of worship that creates and sustains the Christian community. As Saint Augustine put it: we become what we eat. By eating the body of Christ in communion, we become the Body of Christ, the Church. Christ present in the Eucharist remains present in the ongoing life of the Christian community.

Regular participants in the Eucharistic liturgy can give personal testimony to its nourishing power. "Worshipping with kindred souls reminds me that I am not alone on the spiritual journey." "Some Sundays I feel like the homily was directed at me and my struggles to be a faithful Christian." "The upbeat music at my parish lifts my soul in prayer." "When the priest elevates the host, my heart rejoices in the presence of the Lord." "After receiving communion, my prayer to Christ is for strength to make it through the coming week." "The liturgy of the Word gives me something to chew on." "Weekly Mass is crucial to my spiritual growth." "The liturgy encourages me to keep working for justice and peace in our troubled world."

> What could I do to get more out of the Sunday Liturgy?

114. How does the Ascension impact my spiritual life?

In Mark's Ascension account, Jesus commissions his disciples to go into the whole world and proclaim the gospel to every creature: "So then the Lord Jesus, after he had spoken to them, was taken up into heaven and sat down at the right hand of God. And they went out and proclaimed the good news everywhere, while the Lord worked with them and confirmed the message by the signs that accompanied it" (Mark 16: 15-20).

This Gospel passage suggests that we think of the Ascension not as a sad departure of the Lord from his disciples, but as the establishment of a new order where he is present to all people in all times and places through his gift of the Spirit. He is now at the right hand of the Father as the source and mediator of divine truth and energy.

Eyes of faith detect his presence in ways both striking and ordinary. We see Christ's abiding presence in the life of Saint Mother Teresa, who heard the Lord's call to care for the poorest of the poor on the streets of Calcutta and continued this mission, with a smile on her face, for almost five decades. Remarkably she persevered in her vocation even though for almost all of that time she felt totally abandoned by Christ—a fact first made public ten years after her death, when her private letters to her spiritual advisers were published. The revelation of her painful spiritual desolation has made her, paradoxically, an even more compelling example of trust in the continuing presence of the exalted Christ, who works in ways powerful but often mysterious.

As the canonization process of Saint Oscar Romero, archbishop of San Salvador, moved forward, more people learned of the ways Christ worked through him to carry on his mission of preaching the good news to the poor and liberating the oppressed. At one time considered a friend and ally of the wealthy ruling class in El Salvador, Bishop Romero became a courageous public champion of the poor and oppressed. The day after an especially strong condemnation of government violence against "our tormented people," he was killed on March 24, 1980 by a single rifle shot while celebrating Mass. Millions of people in Latin America and around the world venerate him as a martyr for justice, an example of the transforming power of Christ present in oppressed people everywhere and in the lives of all individual believers.

These striking examples of modern Christian discipleship not only make the Ascension claims about Jesus more credible but also prompt further reflection on ways the exalted Christ is present and active in our own lives—perhaps in ways quite ordinary.

> Can I think of a simple example of how the ascended Christ has touched my life?

115. Where can I find energy for my spiritual life?

Let us reflect on Luke's version of the feeding of the multitude, a miracle reported six different times in the Gospels. Jesus spent the day with a large crowd telling them about the kingdom of God and curing their sick. As the day drew to a close, the Twelve suggested to Jesus that he dismiss the crowd so they could go to the surrounding villages and farms to find lodging and provisions. Jesus replied: "You give them something to eat," but the disciples pointed out that they had only five loaves and two fish. At this point, Jesus had the crowd sit in groups of about fifty, said a blessing over the five loaves and two fish, and had the disciples share them with the crowd. They all ate and were satisfied. The leftover fragments filled twelve wicker baskets (Luke 9: 11-17).

We hear this Gospel as a Eucharistic people. The Catholic tradition puts great emphasis on gathering weekly to share the sacred meal of bread and wine. We believe Christ is present at Mass in the assembly, in the proclamation of the scriptural word, and in the consecrated bread and wine. Vatican II taught us that the liturgy is the font and summit of the Christian life. In the Eucharist, we offer prayers of thanksgiving to the Father; we remember the life, death, and resurrection of Christ; and we pledge to carry on his mission, empowered by the Holy Spirit.

This passage from Luke highlights the nourishing function of the Eucharist. Sharing in the sacred meal strengthens us for the journey and energizes us for the task of spreading the reign of God in the world. Receiving communion builds up our immune system against the demonic forces and activates our creative juices for doing good in the world.

We can imagine individuals responding in diverse positive ways to Luke's story of the miraculous feeding. A married man going through a mid-life crisis prays to Christ after receiving communion to help him remain faithful to his marriage vows. A collegian understands her "Amen" when receiving communion as a commitment to share in the mission of Christ to transform the world. An elderly man views his weekly participation in the Eucharistic meal as food for the final part of his journey to God. A mother of three young children finds that Sunday Mass helps her make it through the week.

What could I do to get more out of Sunday Mass?

116. How can I better manage Christmas busyness?

Sometimes, it seems that busyness is a national disease. We Americans work more hours than citizens of Germany and Japan. The better people are at their jobs, the more time they are expected to work. Our middle-class children are involved in so many activities that require the time and attention of parents that fathers and mothers often function like taxi drivers. The ordinary demands of life are multiplied during the Christmas season, with shopping for presents, putting up decorations, preparing special meals, and sending out greeting cards.

Much of this activity has a positive function: keeping alive traditions, attending to the needs to others, having fun, and building community. On the other hand, this glut of external activity can dull our spirits and divert our attention from the inner life of the soul. Busyness can distract us from listening to the Spirit that speaks to us in the inner sanctuary of conscience. The extra demands of the Christmas season can make it even more difficult to find time for prayer and reflection. Oddly, the Advent-Christmas season, filled with great spiritual resources, can actually retard our spiritual growth if we allow busyness to overwhelm the deeper meaning of the liturgical celebrations.

Let us reflect on the familiar story of Joseph in Matthew's Gospel with the challenge of busyness in mind (Matthew 1: 18-24). Joseph is faced with a heart-wrenching situation. He is legally married to Mary but has not yet taken her to his home and consummated the marriage. When he learns she is pregnant, he can imagine only two possibilities: adulterous infidelity or rape. Being a compassionate man, he decides to divorce Mary quietly, trying as much as possible to spare her public punishment and personal ridicule. At this point, an angel of the Lord appears to Joseph in a dream, telling him not to be afraid to take Mary into his home and complete their marriage. The angel explains that this child is of the Holy Spirit and gives Joseph the task of giving the infant the name Jesus, indicating his role as savior of his people. Matthew records no memorable words of Joseph, but simply tells us he did as commanded and took Mary into his home.

In stressful circumstances, Joseph remained attentive to his inner life and open to a word from the Lord. Following the good example of his namesake, the Israelite patriarch Joseph who interpreted dreams for the Egyptian Pharaoh, he recognized dreams as a medium of divine communication. After the birth of Jesus, Joseph once again hears God speaking to him through a dream and takes his family to Egypt to escape the murderous intent of Herod. We can think of Joseph as a man with a rich spiritual life, open to all forms of divine communication in his ordinary life.

Joseph encourages us to develop our inner life so we can withstand the assaults of the busy life and be on alert for a word from God. Some suggestions: be extra attentive to the beautiful liturgical readings during the Advent-Christmas season; carve out time for spiritual reading; say more brief prayers throughout the busy days; see Christ in the people who cross our path; and thank God for the wonderful blessings of this Advent-Christmas season.

How can I tap the spiritual riches of the Advent season?

117. What can I learn by reflecting on Matthew's version of the Passion?

"My God, my God, why have you forsaken me?" The evangelist Matthew, echoing his source the Gospel of Mark, places this lament from Psalm 22 on the lips of Jesus in his death agony on the cross. This cry of anguish epitomizes the abandonment and isolation Jesus suffered throughout his passion: rejected by the religious leaders; betrayed by Judas; abandoned by his disciples; and denied by Peter (Matthew 26). By being especially attentive to these abandonment scenes, we may find new spiritual insights in the familiar Passion story, as the following composite examples suggest.

Jamie, a high school religion teacher, reflects on the scene where Peter, James, and John fall asleep after Jesus asks them to keep watch with him as he prays. She decides to do her daily fifteen minutes of prayer in the morning when she is more awake, rather than in the evening when she is drowsy.

Gus, a married man, who is in the beginning stages of an affair with a co-worker, is struck by the treachery of Judas betraying Jesus with a kiss, and vows to end the affair and concentrate on establishing a better relationship with his wife.

Katie, an empathetic social worker, was turned off by the Mel Gibson movie *The Passion* that seemed to present Jesus as a masochist, is taken with the triple denial of Jesus by Peter. She imagines the disappointment of Jesus, who worked so hard to strengthen Peter's faith, and prays that she can handle the disappointing aspects of her work with unreformed clients while maintaining hope that her efforts are worthwhile.

Ben, a cradle Catholic, is super critical of American bishops not in tune with the spirit of Pope Francis. He notes that the chief priests and the elders totally rejected Jesus and handed him over to Pilate to be executed. Perhaps, he thinks, I am overly harsh on the bishops. After all, they have not rejected Jesus. They are struggling, like I am, to be faithful to the Gospel. They do not have all the answers, nor do I. Ben concludes his brief reflection with a decision to pray regularly for the bishops, who he realizes have a tough job.

Lydia, a lifelong Catholic with a strong sense of the divinity of Christ, feels compelled to reflect on the implication of the lament of Jesus addressed to God, "why have you forsaken me?" Jesus must have felt abandoned by God in his agony. He went to his death in darkness as do we. He had human emotions like us. He knew the joy of friendship and the pain of estrangement. We can identify with Jesus because he was indeed like us in all things but sin. As Lydia ponders these implications of the agonized cry of Jesus on the cross, she comes to a new appreciation of the humanity of Jesus, who is not only true God but also true man. She senses that her spiritual life will be greatly enhanced if she can identify with Jesus in his full humanity while still continuing to adore him as her Lord.

> Does the abandoned Jesus of Matthew's passion have a specific message for me?

118. Do I see Mary as a model of discipleship?

In his Gospel, Luke introduces us to a young woman from Nazareth in Galilee by the name of Mary. Committed to doing the will of God, she consented to be the mother of the Messiah and is now making a hasty trip of some sixty miles to visit her relative Elizabeth, who in old age is six months pregnant. When she arrives, Elizabeth, filled with the Holy Spirit, blesses Mary, extolling her for her faith that God's word would be fulfilled (Luke 1: 39-43).

Mary of Nazareth has been an important figure in Catholic spirituality throughout the whole history of Christianity. She has been a model and inspiration for various groups: vowed religious who dedicate their lives to prayer and service; mothers committed to raising their children; wives determined to hold their families together; contemporary women interested in overcoming the injustices of patriarchy and sexism. Vatican II introduced a broader understanding of Mary as the model for the whole Church and a guide for all men and women striving to be faithful disciples of Christ.

We can envision a Marian influence on Christians serious about following Christ. A man making a career change spends time in prayerful discernment, as did Mary, asking himself relevant questions about potential employers, including their ethical standards and social commitments. A single woman in her late twenties, who was feeling lonely and depressed without a husband, looks to Mary for guidance and decides to make the most of her life: enjoying her friends, advancing her career, participating in her parish, and serving her community. All this activity fills up some empty space, lifts her spirits, and provides her with a sense of meaning and purpose, which leaves her better prepared for a future relationship. Reflecting on the haste with which Mary went to visit Elizabeth, a young man who had completely ignored the Advent season, vows to make the most of the few days before Christmas by setting aside time each day for spiritual reading and acts of charity.

> How can I incorporate lessons learned from
> Mary into my daily life?

119. What spiritual guidance can I get from the man born blind?

John the Evangelist invites reflection on a long, carefully constructed story that begins with Jesus curing a man born blind and goes on to portray his gradual spiritual enlightenment—as well as the spiritual blindness of the Pharisees, who are upset that Jesus healed the man on the Sabbath (John 9: 1-41). We can hear this story as an invitation to examine our own spiritual blindness, bolstered by confidence in the power of Christ to help us see more clearly.

It is helpful to consider a broad range of possible blind spots that inhibit our spiritual growth: not recognizing our own virtues and strengths or our faults and sins; unaware of the needs or the gifts of our family members; blind to the struggles or the accomplishments of friends and colleagues; insensitive to the needs or the virtues of the poor and those living on the margins; not appreciating the power of institutions to oppress people or to contribute to a more just society. By their very nature, blind spots are difficult to detect and often harder to admit and overcome.

Despite a direct challenge from Jesus, the Pharisees in the Gospel remain imprisoned in their spiritual blindness, trapped by their legalistic mentality and fear of losing power. As such, their spiritual blindness symbolizes the common temptation to prefer the darkness of our own limited outlook to the expansive perspective of Christ that illumines our darkness. By way of contrast, the man cured of his physical blindness responds to the invitation of Jesus and becomes more spiritually insightful. He progressively sees Jesus as a prophet, a man from God, and the Son of Man worthy of worship.

We can imagine individuals, suffering from spiritual blindness, who have been enlightened by Christ. Reflecting on Christ's teaching on love of neighbor, a high-powered advertising agent realizes that she has been neglecting her friends and must be more responsive to their needs. While making a retreat centered on Christ's compassion, a man battling poor self-esteem feels more positive about himself and his gifts. After hearing a lecture on Christ as the cosmic Lord, a senior citizen decides he must be more attentive to environmental concerns. Responding to a talk by a former gang member, an affluent suburbanite decides to learn more about the urban poor, who have been largely invisible to her. Praying to the Lord about her intention to marry a guy with a drinking problem, a young woman realizes that her fear of being alone was propelling her into an unwise marriage.

Do these examples help me detect one of my own blind spots, while encouraging me to look to Christ for healing and enlightenment?

120. What can I learn about faith from the Samaritan woman?

In John's Gospel, Jesus and the Samaritan woman engage in a fascinating conversation that led to her conversion and, we might surmise, brought joy to the Lord, who finally found someone receptive to the deeper meaning of his message (John 4: 5-42). What can we learn about the spiritual life from this remarkable woman?

First, the Samaritan woman encourages us to persevere in the spiritual quest despite our fears. At various times in the encounter with Jesus she could have given into her fears and withdrawn: when Jesus, a Jewish male whom she feared might assault her, first broke social taboos by speaking to her; when he challenged her superficial understanding of living water; and when he brought up her personal life by noting her five husbands. In each case, the woman resists the temptation to halt the process and remains in dialogue with Jesus. We all know something of the temptation to abandon the spiritual quest due to our fears: afraid of new demands, cynical about ever making progress, doubtful if the effort to grow spiritually is worthwhile. The Samaritan woman says to us hang in there, don't give up, stay responsive to Christ.

Second, the woman reminds us to look for the deeper meaning of the Gospel message by moving beyond literal interpretations. When she first hears Jesus talking about giving her living water, she notes that he does not have a bucket, but by the end of the story she has a deeper appreciation of the power of the Spirit, the true living water.

We are all blessed with Christ's gift of the Holy Spirit, but we can misunderstand this Spirit as a non-renewable resource, like water that can run out, like spouses who think if they give themselves totally to each other they will have nothing left for themselves, or like those who feel that their service to the poor can only be draining. As the woman at the well came to realize, however, the living water is actually a renewable resource. The more we share the gift of the Spirit the more it multiplies. Love shared is love deepened. Genuine service can be mutually enriching. Sharing the good news roots it more deeply in mind and heart.

Finally, the Samaritan woman urges us to continue to grow in our understanding of Christ and our commitment to his cause. In first encountering Jesus, she saw him as just another Jewish man. As the story develops, she comes to a progressively deeper understanding of him as a prophet who knew her heart, then as the long-awaited Messiah, and finally as the savior of the world. Her example invites us to consider some possible ways of expanding our understanding of Christ and deepening our response to him. We could meditate on an intriguing image of the Lord: for example, the man for others who calls us to a life of service; the icon who reveals the glory of the Lord; the parable of God who instructs us in the realities of the kingdom; the wisdom of the Father who manifests the divine plan; the cosmic Lord who encourages us to care for the earth; or the trustworthy companion who shares the human adventure with us. If this meditation expands our relationship to Christ, we can thank the Samaritan woman for being such a wise spiritual guide.

What specific image of Christ most attracts me and how could I incorporate it into my daily life?

121. What spiritual direction does Cleopas provide?

In Luke's beautifully constructed story of the Road to Emmaus, we find Cleopas and his companion fleeing from Jerusalem (Luke 24: 13-35). They are fearful and deeply disappointed because they had hoped that Jesus, a mighty prophet, was going to free Israel from Roman domination. With the death of Jesus, their disappointment was so overwhelming they could find no hope in reports of an angelic vision claiming Jesus was alive.

In Cleopas we can recognize the common problem of unrealistic expectations, dashed hopes, and deep disappointments, as these personal comments suggest. A black police officer: "I had the overblown expectation that the election of a black president would solve our racial problems." An alcoholic: "After so many failures, I no longer believe I can control my drinking problem on my own." A husband: "My expectations for an untroubled, happy marriage were so unrealistic and my disappointments so great that I now have trouble imagining a better future for our relationship." A female executive: "My expectation was to zoom up the corporate ladder, and then I hit a glass ceiling, leaving me stunned."

On the flight to Emmaus, Cleopas encounters the risen Christ, who explains the Scriptures to him, emphasizing that the Messiah had to suffer. Reaching Emmaus, Christ shares a meal with his hosts, during which "he took bread, blessed and broke it, and gave it to them." With that, Cleopas and his companion recognize him, but he vanishes from their sight. They immediately returned to Jerusalem, where they share the good news with the other disciples that Christ was made known to them in "the breaking of the bread."

For us the story provides perspective and encouragement as we deal with the disappointments of failed expectations and dashed hopes. Not all expectations are realistic. Disappointments are woven into the fabric of real life. Jesus himself had to deal with disappointments, including his failure to convert Israel as a whole and his inability to prepare his disciples for his death. The Scriptures teach us, however, that God, always faithful to the divine promises, can transform failures into victories. Only God can fulfill our deepest hopes. We dare not make an idol out of any of our expectations.

When we gather for Eucharist, we hope to recognize the crucified and risen Lord in the breaking of the bread, as did Cleopas. Christ has the power to raise our dashed hopes and transform our disappointments. Again, we can hear personal testimonies. A social activist: "The Emmaus story gave me new energy for doing my part to promote racial harmony without expecting utopia." A collegian: "After hearing the Gospel, I decided to join AA to deal with my addiction to alcohol." A husband: "In discussing the Gospel after Mass, my wife and I decided to set time aside each week to talk about our hopes for a better marriage." A struggling teacher: "Praying after communion, the thought came to me that the Christ who transformed Cleopas can help me deal with setbacks in my career."

> What is the main lesson I can learn from
> the Emmaus story?

122. What impresses me most about Mary of Magdala?

In the Gospel of Luke, Mary of Magdala plays a prominent role. Luke alone tells us that Jesus cast several demons out of her, indicating that he cured her of a serious illness. She, in turn, traveled with Jesus, along with other women from Galilee, on his missionary journeys, ministering to his needs and supporting his mission. Present at the crucifixion and death of Jesus, she saw where Joseph of Arimathea buried him. On Sunday morning, Mary with her women friends from Galilee came to the tomb to anoint the body of Jesus, but his body was not there. Two men in dazzling garments, presumably angels, told them Jesus had been raised as he foretold. Mary and her friends returned from the tomb and announced their story to the eleven, but they did not believe them. Peter went to the tomb and saw the body was gone. Luke tells us he was amazed but does not say he believed (Luke 24: 1-12).

Luke presents Mary Magdalene as the first witness to the resurrection and the first to announce the good news to others, providing the basis for her title "Apostle to the Apostles." In this role, she serves as an example for all Christians of our common responsibility to testify to our faith in the risen Christ and share the good news with others. As Mary's story suggests, giving effective testimony to resurrection faith can be difficult, because people are not always ready to receive the message. Historically, Christianity spread by the supreme witness of the martyrs who gave their lives for their faith, and our own experience suggests that personal example is a more effective witness than words alone. The Easter message, therefore, resonates with others when believers live it out on a daily basis. We can honor Mary Magdalene by persevering in our "testimony of action" to the risen Christ, even when it seems fruitless.

Some examples of faithful witness to the risen Christ: a teacher spends extra time with her sixth-grade student who comes from a troubled home and has trouble paying attention in class; a secretary maintains a joyful spirit at work even when dealing with a grumpy boss; a father periodically tells his teenage son he prays to the risen Lord to help him be a better father; grandparents, strengthened by their faith in Christ, are raising two children of their daughter who is emotionally unable to care for them.

How could I become a better witness to my faith in the risen Lord?

123. What does Doubting Thomas teach me about faith?

Thomas, called the "Twin," was a disciple of Jesus who expressed doubts about where his Master intended to go. He has worked his way into our common vocabulary as Doubting Thomas. Absent when the risen Christ appeared to the other disciples, Thomas wanted empirical proof before he was ready to believe. Blessed with a personal encounter with the risen Lord, Thomas made a profound statement of belief: "My Lord and my God" (John 20: 19-31).

Thomas can be a guide for us as we deal with the doubts that impact our spiritual life. Some doubts have a more academic character: for example, how reliable are the appearance accounts in the Gospels, including this one featuring Thomas? The work of theologians and scripture scholars, available in popular books, lectures, and classes, can help with such academic questions. Other doubts arise from the various trials of life that test our faith, like "gold tested by fire" (see 1 Peter 1:17), and raise questions about the power, efficacy, wisdom, and relevance of faith in the resurrection of Christ. Facing such doubts, John's Gospel story about Thomas can speak to our situation, as Jesus himself suggested: "Blessed are those who have not seen and have believed."

We can imagine composite stories of Easter faith overcoming doubts raised by the crosses of life. A religious sister, professed over thirty years, is troubled by her inability to deepen her prayer life, especially since she finds little consolation in prayer. Reflecting on the story of Doubting Thomas, she hears the Lord speaking to her: "Blessed are those who experience no consolation in prayer and still believe in the importance and power of prayer." A recent college graduate has endured three unsuccessful job interviews and is losing confidence in himself and his ability to find meaningful work. He finds renewed hope for himself by recalling how Jesus eventually got Thomas, with all his doubts and failures, to understand and accept his vocation as a disciple. A man recently divorced for the second time is feeling like a failure, burdened by guilt over his role in both breakups. He imagines the various emotions Thomas experienced: a painful self-loathing when he faced his cowardly abandonment of his Master at the time of his arrest; a deep sadness when he learned that Jesus was convicted, crucified, and died; and an indescribable joy when he heard the words of the risen Lord: "Peace be with you." Perhaps, it is still possible, the man concludes, for a twice-divorced person to be forgiven and to find new purpose and meaning in life. An independent-minded single mother, working full time to support her two children, feels isolated and begins to doubt that she can continue to meet her responsibilities by herself. When she reflects on how Thomas related to the other disciples, moving from a sense of isolation and estrangement from them when they told him about seeing the risen Lord to joyful union with them after his own transforming experience. Somehow that insight convinces the mother she has to be more accepting of the support offered by family and friends.

Identifying specific ways that the crosses of life challenge our faith prepares us to encounter the risen Lord and to say with Thomas, "My Lord and my God."

> What is my own biggest challenge to faith and how can Thomas help me deal with it?

124. What can I learn about humility from John the Baptist?

The evangelist Mark begins his Gospel by introducing us to John the Baptist (Mark 1: 1-8). Quoting the prophet Isaiah, he presents John as God's messenger, a voice crying out in the desert: "Prepare the way of the Lord." Dressed like the prophet Elijah,

John proclaims the coming of the mighty one who will baptize with the Holy Spirit. The Baptist is not the Messiah, but he has the crucial task of preparing the way for God's anointed One.

As Christians, we believe that life is filled with opportunities to encounter the Christ who is our constant companion on the journey. John the Baptist can help us prepare for those encounters with the Lord so they can be more fruitful. His austere lifestyle in the desert suggests that self-discipline helps clear the way for recognizing the Lord's presence in our lives. For example, a middle-aged woman begins eating properly and exercising regularly and discovers she is more attuned to the presence of Christ in her family and friends.

As an essential element in his baptism by water, John insisted on repentance for the forgiveness of sins, reminding us that our sins can blind us to the presence of Christ in our lives. For example, a young married man who is addicted to Internet pornography, sees what is happening to him and kicks the habit, which enables him to be more attentive to Christ present in his wife and children.

The Baptist's remarkable ability to put aside his own ego and ambitions in order to concentrate on his task of preparing the way for the Messiah, challenges us to keep our own interests in reasonable check so we can attend to the needs of others. For example, a retired accountant, often driven by a self-serving pride, starts visiting seniors in a nursing home, discovering to his surprise the simple joy of listening to others without trying to impress them.

John lived his whole life in expectation of the coming of the Lord, which enabled him to identify Jesus when he came to be baptized, suggesting to us that anticipating an encounter with Christ helps make it more fruitful. For example, a faithful Catholic who attends Mass regularly is getting more out of the liturgy now that she expects to meet Christ not just in the consecrated bread and wine but also in the assembly and the scripture readings.

Which advice of John the Baptist would be my best
next step: be disciplined; repent of sins; set aside ego;
or expect to encounter Christ in new ways?

125. What can I learn about discernment from Mary?

The evangelist Luke has passed on to us the familiar story known as the Annunciation. The Angel Gabriel appears to a young girl in Nazareth, by the name of Mary, announcing she is to give birth to a son who will rule over the house of Jacob forever. After getting a clarification from Gabriel about how this is going to happen, Mary responds: "Let it be with me according to your word" (Luke 1: 26-38).

As Vatican II taught, Mary serves as the exemplar of Christian discipleship, a model for following Christ. In this Gospel passage, Mary, initially troubled by the angel's greeting, listens to the message, asks an appropriate question, and responds wholeheartedly with a commitment to do God's will. As baptized Christians, we are all called by God to follow Christ intelligently and with full dedication, as did Mary.

We can imagine examples of individual Christians following Mary's example by asking fitting questions that lead to more effective discipleship. Lisa lost her beloved husband to cancer at age 26, leaving her with two young children to raise by herself. For about six months, she was deeply depressed and not functioning well as a mother. She was constantly asking God why her soulmate had been taken from her so soon. One night, while saying the Rosary in bed, it occurred to Lisa that there was no good answer to why her husband died so young, and that the right question was not why, but how: how to cope with her situation and meet her responsibilities as a mother. Changing the question from "why" to "how" enabled her to manage her sadness and give proper attention to her children.

Gerry, a lifelong Catholic, faithful husband, a regular at Sunday Mass, focused his practice of the faith on meeting the minimum requirements. His fundamental questions were about what was necessary to get to heaven, to remain in good standing with the Church, and to maintain respectability in the community. One Sunday he heard a homily at Mass that emphasized Mary's generous response to God's call at the Annunciation. The deacon said all Christians are called not just to avoid hell but to share generously in the mission of Christ. Something about Mary's good example struck Gerry, and he began to ask himself not about minimum requirements but about how he could grow spiritually and do more to make the world a better place.

> Following Mary's example, what question should I ask myself to take the next step forward on my spiritual journey?

126. What does the Canaanite woman teach me about faith?

In his Gospel, Matthew presents the Canaanite woman as a model of preserving faith (Matthew 15: 21-28). In contrast to the Jewish leaders, who rejected him and his disciples who do not understand him, the woman had unwavering faith that Jesus could heal her daughter, who is tormented by a demon. Even when Jesus rebuffed her initial plea for help by insisting that his mission is to his fellow Jews and not to Gentile dogs like her, she persisted by cleverly arguing that even dogs eat the scraps that fall from the table of their masters. Impressed with the great faith of this Gentile woman, Jesus extended the scope of his mission and healed her daughter.

The Canaanite woman can tutor us in the ways of faith. First of all, she reminds us that Christian faith recognizes Jesus as the Savior, the one who heals and reconciles. At the most fundamental level, faith is not first of all about giving intellectual assent to a series of truths, but involves a heartfelt commitment to Jesus Christ, the risen Lord, who shares his healing Spirit with us.

A cradle Catholic, who took into adulthood a very legalistic understanding of his faith as keeping a collection of moral prohibitions in order to save his soul, made a retreat focused on developing a more personal relationship to Christ. The experience set the man on a spiritual path that transformed his heavy moralistic sense of Catholicism into a more joyful commitment to Christ, who calls him to a life of generous Christian discipleship. We could say that he came to know what the Canaanite woman knew instinctively, that Christ is our primary hope for a fulfilled life.

Secondly, the Canaanite woman serves as a model of a steadfast faith that perseveres despite obstacles. Personal commitment to Christ inevitably encounters a variety of challenges: sickness and death; sins and failures; rejections and estrangements; misunderstanding and ridicule. The woman, who persisted despite an initial rejection by Jesus, encourages us to persevere in our faith despite all obstacles, confident that Christ possesses remarkable saving power. By continuing to bet our lives on Christ, we maintain an open heart that is receptive to his healing power.

A woman who describes herself as a gay Catholic feminist has often felt rejected by her Catholic Church, both as a woman and as a lesbian. Nevertheless, she is determined not to leave the Church, because it remains her best resource for staying in touch with the teaching and power of Christ. For her, the Gentile woman is a great inspiration, the prime Gospel model of persistent faith, more attuned to Christ and his power than his Jewish male disciples.

> What is the next step I could take to deepen my relationship with Christ?

127. How does John the Baptist encourage me to persevere in doing good?

Matthew's Gospel catches John the Baptist in a vulnerable moment of doubt (Matthew 11: 2-11). We know John as a strong, disciplined, resolute prophet: conceived miraculously and named by the angel Gabriel; lived as an ascetic in the desert preaching a baptism of repentance; delivered an uncompromising call for personal conversion; baptized Jesus, but unselfishly ceded leadership of the reform movement to him; and publicly denounced Herod for marrying his brother's wife, Herodias, which landed him in prison and eventually cost him his life. Languishing in prison, the resolute precursor has his moments of doubt. Did he hand over leadership to the right person? Is Jesus too soft and accommodating? Is he really the awaited Messiah, or should we look for another?

The example of the vulnerable Baptist frees us for honest reflection on any doubts we may have about persevering in doing good. A mother who has been praying for years that her son kick his drug habit wonders if praying does any good. A young woman with high standards of sexual morality contemplates abandoning her ideals in order to please a boyfriend. A man who periodically helps a friend in need considers abandoning the practice because the friend seldom says thanks. A wife who usually seeks reconciliation after an argument with her husband plans a spiteful silence until he admits his fault in the dispute. A collegian who studies hard and gets below-average grades is discouraged and tempted to cut back on his study time. A peace activist who has participated in many protests against war fears it has all been for naught. John invites all these people—and all of us—to reflect on ways we are tempted, like the Baptist briefly was, to give up on following Christ and his call to high ideals.

Responding to John's doubt, Jesus tells the messengers to report the healing miracles he has been working: the blind see, the lame walk, lepers are cleansed, the deaf hear, even the dead are raised. Jesus is recalling the signs that Isaiah connected with the saving presence of God, who will strengthen the hands that are feeble, make firm the knees that are weak and make strong hearts that are frightened. The reign of God is often hidden and easy to miss, but it has amazing power to strengthen our resolve.

The response of Jesus to the Baptist speaks to our doubting hearts: keep praying; persevere in doing good; maintain your high ideals; trust the Gospel promises; be alert for signs of progress; concentrate more on effort than success; do what is right even if there is no clear payoff; and remain steadfast in seeking justice and peace.

> Can I think of a time when Christ helped me perservere in a challenging situation?

128. What can I learn about repentance from John the Baptist?

In his Gospel, Luke introduces us in a different way from Mark to the compelling figure or John the Baptist (Luke 3: 1-6). In Luke's version, John appears at a particular time in world history, when Tiberius Caesar was in his fifteenth year as emperor of Rome and Pontius Pilate was governor of Judea, in charge of the Roman occupation of the land of the Jews which began in 63 BC. Born into a priestly Jewish family, John is living an ascetic life in the Judean desert. Inspired by the word of God and fulfilling a prophesy of Isaiah, he goes about the region of the Jordan River proclaiming "a baptism of repentance for the forgiveness of sins." Luke interprets the mission of John with the poetic prophesy of Isaiah: "The voice of one crying out in the wilderness: Prepare the way of the Lord . . . and 'all flesh shall see the salvation of God.'"

John's call for repentance suggests a radical conversion, a change of heart, a transformation of fundamental attitudes, a turning away from sin, and an embrace of God's will. This kind of personal repentance has social consequences leading to a more fulfilled life, more harmonious relationships, a more humane culture, a more just society, and a more peaceful world.

We can envision some positive responses to the message of John the Baptist. A professor who often felt inferior to his learned colleagues, came to a greater appreciation of his own God-given gifts, enabling him to function with greater confidence. A wife who was often frustrated by her husband's reluctance to express his feelings, developed a greater appreciation of his non-verbal expressions of love, which greatly improved their marriage. A young man once proud of his many sexual conquests learned to see women not as objects to be used but as persons to be treasured, which led him to repent of his sins and commit himself to forming healthier relationships based on mutual respect. An engineer who liked to make fun of what he called "tree-hugging" environmentalists, listened to Pope Francis and decided to use his skills to help conserve energy.

> What is the main transformation I need in my life and how can I begin the process of repentance?

129. What advice can I glean from the story of Zacchaeus?

Only Luke tells us the endearing story of Zacchaeus, a wealthy chief tax collector who heard Jesus was passing through Jericho and wanted to see who he was. Short in stature and unable to see Jesus because of the crowd, he climbs a sycamore tree to catch sight of him as he passes by. Jesus spots him and says: "Zacchaeus, hurry and come down; for I must stay at your house today."

The crowd is upset that Jesus would stay with such a disreputable sinner who has grown wealthy by collaborating with their Roman oppressors. For his part, Zacchaeus is a changed man, telling Jesus he will give half of his vast wealth to the poor and repay fourfold those he extorted. Jesus responds that salvation has come to Zacchaeus today for the "Son of Man has come to seek out and to save what was lost" (Luke 19: 1-10).

Reflecting on the details of the story of Zacchaeus, we can discern advice and encouragement for our own spiritual journey. By taking advantage of Jesus passing through Jericho, Zacchaeus reminds us of the importance of seizing the moment, making the most of opportunities, and being alert to the Lord passing our way. By climbing a tree, he encourages us to seek out Christ and to look for creative ways to encounter him. By his immediate joyful response to Jesus, he warns us against procrastination and instructs us in the joy of discipleship. His conversion invites us to look for ways to grow closer to Christ intellectually, morally, and spiritually. His wholehearted commitment to restitution encourages our own efforts to heal relationships and work for justice.

Christians serious about spiritual growth can find inspiration in the Zacchaeus story. A retired plumber who has always been faithful to the teachings of his Catholic faith decides he wants to know more about Jesus and spends time each day reading the Gospels. A secretary who has a stressful job plans to be more alert to opportunities to make others feel welcome and important. A husband who is habitually lax in doing his share of the domestic chores makes a resolution to be more responsible in order to show his love for his wife. A salesperson who has been shirking her duties at work decides to spend some extra time at the store making up for missed opportunities.

How could I put inspiration from Zacchaeus into practice?

130. What can I learn about fidelity from Vaclav Maly?

In Luke's Gospel we find the rather shocking statement of Jesus: "I came to bring fire to the earth, and how I wish it were already kindled!" After noting his anguish over his pending passion and death, he adds: "Do you think that I have come to bring peace to the earth? No, I tell you, but rather division!" which will even pit family members against one another (Luke 12: 49-53).

The passage reminds us that the fidelity of Jesus to the cause of God generated opposition from his family and hometown friends as well as the religious and political establishment, which culminated in his death on the cross. Christ's message can serve as a fiery weapon that attacks personal prejudice, family dysfunction, cultural bias, and societal injustice. Historically, Christ's faithful witnesses have run into a firestorm of opposition as the powerful have protected their privileges with violent persecutions and coercive intimidation.

We can, for example, recall the faithful witness of the Czech priest Vaclav Maly, who just a year after his ordination in 1976 signed Charter 77 demanding that the Communist regime respect human rights. Over the next twelve years, Maly was under constant surveillance, arrested and interrogated over 250 times, and on one occasion brutally tortured, all in an effort to make him soften his criticism of the Communist government. Relying totally on Christ, who brought fire to the earth, Father Maly persevered as a faithful witness to Gospel truth, playing a major role in the Velvet Revolution which toppled the government in 1989 and led to the election of the playwright Vaclav Havel. Maly declined the opportunity to participate in the government, opting instead to continue to share in Christ's mission as a priest and later as a bishop.

In a lengthy private conversation with Maly in Prague, he reminded me that Christians in the United States have an obligation to stand up for Gospel truth against the dominating idols of our culture, such as consumerism and individualism. His example encourages us to resist those destructive trends as completely as possible, just as he refused to soften even slightly his criticism of the totalitarian government.

> In what specific ways could I follow the
> courageous example of Maly?

131. What inspiration can I find in the life of Martin Luther King?

After completing his doctorate in theology at Boston University in 1954, Martin Luther King accepted a call to serve as the pastor of the Dexter Avenue Baptist Church in Montgomery, Alabama. Less than a year later, Rosa Parks was arrested for refusing to give up her seat on a bus to a white man. Circumstances propelled King into the leadership of the ensuing Montgomery bus boycott. The long struggle weighed on King as he dealt with the firebombing of his house and several arrests. One night, agitated and unable to sleep, he went to his kitchen to pray over the possibility of resigning as leader of the boycott. While deep in prayerful reflection, he heard an inner voice speaking: "Martin Luther, stand up for righteousness, stand up for justice, stand up for the truth, and lo, I will be with you even until the end of the world." Empowered by this message from Christ, King helped lead the Montgomery bus boycott to a successful conclusion and continued on to labor tirelessly for racial justice and world peace until his assassination in 1968.

Dr. King stands in the tradition of believers who have known the strength of the Lord when weighed down by dark forces. John's Gospel raises up the figure of John the Baptist, who not only testified to Jesus as Lamb of God and Son of God but also received strength and assurance from Christ when plagued with doubts while languishing in Herod's prison (John 1: 29-34). In his first letter to the Corinthian community, which was burdened by internal strife and division, Paul reminds them that they are sanctified in Christ Jesus and called to be holy. He prays that they receive the grace and peace of Christ which can bring reconciliation and unity to their divided community (Corinthians 1: 1-3).

It is not only the well-known, like Dr. King, John the Baptist, and Paul the Apostle, who give witness to the strengthening power of Christ, available to all oppressed by suffering and evil. It is ordinary people in their daily lives. A woman who lost her husband and then was diagnosed with cancer speaks of the miracle of Christ's spirit that has helped her get through it all. A man who has to work two difficult jobs to support his family sometimes wonders how his is surviving and concludes it is only with the Lord's help. A young woman who battles low self-esteem with little emotional support from her parents attributes her growing self-confidence to her faith in Christ. A grandfather who suffers from episodic depression counts on Christ's strength even when he is unable to concentrate on praying. A corporate executive, once weighed down by excessive attention to her job, is now living a more balanced life thanks to her daily meditation on the gospel stories of Jesus.

> Can I recall a time when Christ has lifted me up when oppressed by dark forces?

132. What can I learn about faith from Karl Rahner?

When Jesus identified himself as the Son of Man who had come down from heaven, many of his disciples left him, as John's Gospel tells us. Jesus then asked the Twelve if they also wanted to leave and Peter responded: "Lord, to whom can we go? You have the words of eternal life" adding we are convinced "you are the Holy One of God" (John 6: 60-69).

This passage invites reflection on loyalty to Christ in the contemporary world marked by religious pluralism, competing worldviews, and multiple spiritual options. I want to raise up the German Jesuit theologian Karl Rahner (1904-1984) as an instructive example of maintaining Christian faith in today's postmodern world. Rahner understood the contemporary challenges to faith: more Catholics will leave the Church because they have other live options; the societal and cultural factors that traditionally supported belief will continue to erode; no individual or group can give compelling answers to all the objections to faith in God and, more specifically, to belief in Christ.

At the same time, Rahner offers helpful theological perspectives and insights to deal with these challenges: Christianity is not a philosophy of life or an ethical system, but does involve commitment to the crucified and risen person Jesus Christ; we know that Jesus presented himself as the definitive prophet sent to establish and extend the reign of God—an historical fact that can ground belief in him as the absolute savior; many Christians who have left the Church continue to believe in Christ and may have even deepened their commitment to him.

When Rahner was asked why he remained a Catholic, he responded that he was born one and never found anything that would help him understand better the great realities of love, freedom, suffering, and death; nothing that would help him live more responsibly and nobly. Note that his answer is not abstract or speculative but concrete and practical, much like Peter's response to Jesus. Maintaining his fundamental Christian faith enabled Rahner to grow in his relationship to Christ, so that later in life he was able to throw his arms around Jesus as an expression of love.

What can I learn from the response of Peter and the example of Rahner about maintaining and deepening my faith in Christ?

Chapter Six

Christian Life (living the Gospel)

133. Am I comfortable witnessing to my faith?

In Matthew's Gospel, Jesus addresses us: "You are the light of the world." Then he adds: "let your light shine before others, so that they may see your good works and give glory to your Father in heaven" (Matthew 5: 14-16). Traditionally, we have celebrated a whole host of canonized saints, luminaries like Francis of Assisi and Teresa of Avila, who have let their bright light shine before others.

Vatican II reminds us, however, that all the baptized—not just the famous saints—are responsible for bringing the light of Christ to the world. We are all called to give witness to the faith that illumines our journey. Many Christians are not comfortable with this responsibility or with the language of "giving witness." Some live a private piety that concentrates on personal salvation and leaves little room for serving others and transforming society. Others associate the notion of witness with aggressive fundamentalists who engage in objectionable proselytizing. Many good Catholics especially think that their knowledge of the faith is too limited for them to serve as effective witnesses.

Being a Christian witness in the United States today has its own distinctive challenges. There are a growing number of citizens who claim no religious affiliation, over 20% of the population. Christians now constitute only about half of the total population. One out of every four adult Catholics has left the Church. Almost all Catholics have family members or friends who no longer practice the faith.

The times call for more authentic and credible ways of letting our light shine before others. We can start by striving to be genuine Christians: joyful and fully alive; faithful and hope-filled; compassionate and loving; honest and just. Being a faithful Christian leads to effective witness in everyday life: caring for the less fortunate; contributing to family harmony; maintaining good friendships; being a good neighbor; helping to humanize culture; working for a more just society and peaceful world.

Much of Christian witness occurs in the family setting: spouses helping one another reach their potential; parents forming their children in Gospel values; siblings learning to share and collaborate; grandparents providing perspective and support. Christians can help humanize the worksite by doing an honest day's work, treating colleagues with respect, maintaining professional standards, and exercising creativity. Christians can let their light shine in the public arena by voting intelligently, contributing to charitable causes, supporting legislation that serves the common good, staying informed on public policy issues, participating in cultural events, and celebrating civic holidays.

Sometimes, words strengthen such credible Christian witness. A father tells his teenage son that going to Mass regularly has helped him to be a better parent. An executive explains to a friend at work that she does not participate in the gossip about a colleague because it violates her sense of Christian charity. A parishioner not only contributes to the Catholic Campaign for Human Development but also speaks out against its vocal critics, arguing that it is indeed an effective Christian way to empower the poor. Christ urges all of us to let our light shine by virtuous lives and good deeds and, when appropriate, by timely words.

> How could I be a better witness to my Christian faith?

134. How can I participate more fully in the mission of Christ, the Suffering Servant?

Christian spirituality has to do with putting on the mind of Christ. We grow spiritually by deepening our understanding of Christ and participating more fully in his mission to spread the reign of God. All four gospels describe the baptism of Jesus as a decisive event in his life. After over thirty years of a private life in the obscurity of Nazareth in Galilee, Jesus begins his public ministry by travelling to Judea and associating himself with the reform movement of John the Baptist. Matthew portrays the baptism as a public manifestation of Jesus as God's beloved Son (Matthew 3: 13-17).

Typically, in this story Matthew presents Jesus as the fulfillment of the Hebrew scriptures: he is the new Israel called out of Egypt; the new Moses who ascends the mountain to proclaim the new law; the new David, whose kingdom will be vast and enduring. Matthew's depiction of the baptism of Jesus draws on the image of Isaiah's Suffering Servant who, endowed by God with a gentle and understanding spirit, establishes justice on the earth, serves as a light for the nation, opens the eyes of the blind, and brings out prisoners from confinement. For Matthew, Jesus is the anointed servant of God, the chosen one filled with the divine spirit, called to bring forth justice to the nations. His message is not harsh and judgmental but compassionate and forgiving. Jesus goes about doing good and healing all those oppressed by the devil. Having received the Holy Spirit at his baptism, like a dove descending upon him, he preaches the good news to the poor and liberates those imprisoned by ignorance and sin. By word and example, he demonstrates the healing power of love, compassion, and forgiveness in human affairs—both private and public.

Putting on the mind of Christ, the anointed servant, can lead to personal conversion and deeper commitment. A father who disciplined his children too harshly learns to be more understanding and compassionate. A woman with a private spirituality focused on saving her soul now expresses her faith by visiting the elderly in a nursing home. A man with a boring job finds meaning at work by contributing to a friendlier atmosphere. A young woman on a career path to a high paying job decides to pursue a less lucrative career that enables her to work with the poor. All of us who come to a deeper understanding of Christ, the servant of God, can find better ways of serving others and spreading the kingdom.

> What next step should I take to participate in the mission of Christ?

135. How can I become a more faithful citizen?

Matthew reports that the Pharisees, collaborating with their Herodian political rivals, have set a clever trap for Jesus by asking his opinion on the disputed question of whether or not it is lawful to pay the census tax to Caesar (Matthew 22: 15-21). If Jesus says no, he risks reprisal from the Herodians, who support and benefit from the Roman occupation. If he says yes, he will lose support of the Jews who suffer greatly from the burdensome tax. Jesus cleverly eludes the trap by his well-known, but enigmatic, response: "Give therefore to the emperor the things that are the emperor's, and to God the things that are God's."

We can marvel at the clever response of Jesus, but what does it mean for us today? Clearly, it does not provide specific answers to complicated church and state issues. We can use it, however, to reflect on our general obligations to both God and the state. We owe everything to God, who is the Source of all blessings, the true Lord without rivals. Idol-making is forbidden. We dare not make an absolute out of any finite reality. No Caesar, no state, no government, no nation, no political party can claim our total allegiance. Only God are we to love with all our mind, heart, and soul. God remains the judge of the state and all of its policies and goals.

At the same time, the state has a proper role to play in ordering human affairs and providing for the common good. As citizens we have both rights and responsibilities. Our Christian faith provides guidance and motivation for participating in the political, economic, and cultural life of the country: authentic discipleship includes faithful citizenship; patriotism is a virtue; there is a proper way to love our country. Vatican II called us to act as leaven in society by striving to humanize our world. Rendering to Caesar has its place when governed by our allegiance to God, the just judge.

Christians have diverse ways of becoming more faithful citizens. A couple with two young children living below the government poverty line prays every day for a more just society. A lawyer decides to examine more thoroughly whether the contraceptive mandate of the Affordable Care Act, with its accommodations, really violates the conscience of Catholics or not. A strong pro-life Christian refines the way she expresses her position by avoiding slogans such as "abortion is murder." A factory worker prepares for an upcoming gubernatorial election by comparing the position of the two candidates on the economic issues that concern him most. A woman in her late twenties decides to vote for the first time in her life in a presidential election. A peace activist gets a letter published in the local newspaper questioning the use of drones in the war on ISIS on the grounds that the collateral damage only enhances their recruiting efforts.

> What specific action could I take to become a more effective citizen?

136. How can I cooperate more effectively with the Spirit?

In John's farewell discourse at the Last Supper, Jesus promises his disciples that he will send them the Advocate, the Spirit of Truth, who will testify to himself and will guide them to all truth (John 16: 12-15). As Christians, we believe that Christ has kept his promise. He has not abandoned us, leaving us to make the journey of life on our own. He has sent us the Holy Spirit, the Advocate who guides us to an ever deeper understanding of Jesus and his message. During his earthly life, Jesus carried out his mission under the limitations of time and space. He reached only a tiny percentage of the total population and did not succeed in fully forming his intimate circle of disciples. By sending the Advocate, Jesus extends his mission to the whole world and empowers his disciples to grow in the understanding and practice of their faith.

We see the Advocate at work in the great missionaries who spread the Gospel around the world: for example, the Italian Jesuit Matteo Ricci (1552-1610) who became fluent in Chinese; gained admittance into China; earned the respect of Chinese scholars while adopting their dress and manners; won the favorable attention of the Emperor; demonstrated that Confucian thought was compatible with Christianity and could serve as a prelude for the Gospel; produced a Chinese catechism; developed an indigenous Chinese liturgy; and founded a thriving Christian community.

We can also think of more ordinary examples of Christians who have cooperated with the Advocate in becoming committed, effective disciples of Christ. Thousands of dedicated Catholics now serve as lay ecclesial ministers (for example, pastoral administrators and religious education directors) in parishes all over the world. Countless others, empowered by the Advocate, carry on the mission of Christ by following his example in their everyday lives. For example, prompted by the Spirit, a geology professor decides to read a book by a contemporary scripture scholar on the book of Genesis which assures him that there was no essential conflict between his religious beliefs and evolutionary science. After praying to the Holy Spirit for guidance, a mother finds just the right approach to get her teenage son to see a counselor about his anger problem.

> Can I recall times when the Advocate promised by Christ has guided or strengthened me?

137. How can I keep a healthy perspective on evil in the world?

We are inundated with a lot of bad news about our world today: political gridlock in Washington; racial tensions around the country; wars and violence in the Middle East; infectious disease outbreaks in Latin American and Africa; the threat posed by ISIS and other terror groups—to note only some of the more prominent disturbing situations in our world.

Faced with so much bad news, some people become cynical and pessimistic, convinced that the world is under the control of dark forces. Others try to ignore the distressing news while living comfortably in their own well-ordered part of the world. The evangelist John offers some perspective on the condition of the world, especially in the passage: "Indeed, God did not send the Son into the world to condemn the world, but in order that the world might be saved through him" (John 3: 13-17). In Jesus' teaching, the world is not fated to follow its own destructive inclinations but is the object of divine love, a love so strong that it prompted God to send his only Son so that the people in the world might not perish but might have eternal life. The world is not finally controlled by Satan but is in the hands of a loving God. The presence of sin in the world is all too obvious, but it is always surrounded by the more powerful grace of the Holy Spirit. Evil may seem to be having its way in the world, but the reign of God is always at work, often hidden but eventually triumphant over all the dark forces. The Church lives not apart from the world but in the world, as Vatican II insists, so that its members can be a leaven, humanizing the world from within.

This particular Gospel passage's inspired perspective on the affairs of the world challenges both a bitter cynicism and a comfortable passivity. God's love for the world gives us hope for its future and energizes us to help spread God's reign in the world. For example, a chronically ill woman manages her deep distress over the immense misery in the world by offering her sufferings each day for one specific group of victims, such as Christians in northern Iraq or high school girls taken captive in Nigeria. A senior citizen overcomes his pessimism about current world affairs by recalling totally unexpected positive events in the past, such as the fall of the Berlin Wall, the liberation of Eastern Europe from Soviet domination, and the end of apartheid in South Africa. An affluent couple volunteers regularly at a food distribution center as part of a conscious effort to expand their view of the world and contribute to the wellbeing of their community. A world loved by God deserves our attention and our best efforts to help it actualize its potential for good.

> What small step could I take to help spread God's reign in my part of the world?

138. Am I tempted to rash behavior?

Luke reports Jesus telling his disciples this parable. A rich man fires his steward for squandering his property. Too weak to do manual labor and too ashamed to beg, the steward decides to make friends by reducing the amount debtors owe his master on the hope that they will then welcome him into their homes. The master finds out about his scheme but instead of throwing the dishonest steward in jail, he praises him for acting "shrewdly." Jesus then explains: "For the children of this age are more shrewd in dealing with their own generation than are the children of light" (Luke 16: 1-13).

Scripture scholars are not agreed on how to interpret the parable, but one possibility is that it calls us to be wise, prudent, and clever in becoming better disciples of Christ and sharing more effectively in his mission to spread the kingdom in the world. We know the temptation to act imprudently: neglecting prayer; relying on God without cooperating with divine grace; expecting success without effort; failing to recognize the power of evil forces; making an idol out of wealth and power; thinking we can experience resurrection joy without taking up the cross; hoping for peace without working for justice.

We can imagine individuals responding positively to this interpretation. An affluent retired doctor in the habit of giving a set amount to charitable requests, now investigates the administrative practices of the charities and gives more generously to those which use contributions efficiently. An aunt serving as a confirmation sponsor for her niece reads some articles on the sacrament to prepare herself for conversations with her niece. An economics professor interested in reducing poverty in his community forms a group of colleagues to study the problem and to come up with a couple of concrete suggestions to present to city government. A religious sister struggling to become less judgmental and more tolerant finds a wise spiritual director to help her with the problem.

How could I become a more prudent disciple of Christ?

139. Am I attentive to the needs of those on the margins?

In Luke's Gospel, Jesus tells the Pharisees a story contrasting two men: a rich man, who lived a life of luxury, wearing fine clothes and enjoying sumptuous meal, and Lazarus, a poor man lying at the door of the rich man, who is covered with sores and does not have enough to eat. When Lazarus dies, angels carried him to the bosom of Abraham. When the rich man dies, he ends up in the nether world tormented by flames. The rich man asks Abraham to send Lazarus with a touch of water to cool his tongue, but Abraham says this is impossible because a great chasm prevents passage from one side to the other. Then the man asks Abraham to warn his five brothers so they don't end up in torment, but the great patriarch points out they had Moses and the prophets to guide them and if they would not listen to them, "Neither will they be convinced even if someone rises from the dead" (Luke 16: 19-31).

Why was the rich man punished? It was not simply because he had great wealth. Nor had he done anything to hurt Lazarus such as having him arrested for loitering or removed as a danger to public health. The real sin of the rich man was ignoring Lazarus, failing to meet his responsibility to assist a fellow Jew in need, and violating the covenant of love that created solidarity among all Jews.

For many of us in the United States today, it seems easy to ignore the poor, since they are often out of sight. Even though around 45 million Americans live below the government poverty line (about 14 percent of the total population), rich and middle-class people can go long periods without encountering someone they know is poor. This parable tells us that contemporary Christians, who believe all human beings are members of God's family, have a moral responsibility to listen attentively for cries of the poor and assist them in concrete ways.

Some suggestions. Participate in the Catholic Campaign for Human Development by reading their informational material on poverty in the United States and by contributing generously to fund self-help programs for poor persons—not a hand out but a way out. Join Bread for the World, an interfaith group that lobbies Congress to pass legislation that helps those living below the poverty line. Volunteer to serve at a food distribution center. Make a conscious effort to befriend a poor person. Help unemployed friends and parishioners find a job. Tutor an inner-city child in reading. Get your parish to tithe the weekly collection to help needy groups. Join Habitat for Humanity and help build a house for a low-income family. Get involved in a local charity that includes personal interactions with poor persons. Think creatively of other options.

> What can I realistically do to help people trapped in the hellish circle of poverty?

140. Are my actions consistent and authentic?

The evangelist Matthew invites us to explore the relationship between words and deeds. A father asks his two sons to go work in the vineyards: one says no but then changes his mind and goes; the other says yes but does not go. Jesus then asks which one did the will of the father (Matthew 21: 28-32). We would probably choose, as did the Jewish religious leaders, the one who changed his mind and actually went and worked in the vineyard. With that response, we affirm the value of doing the right thing and putting into practice our Christian faith. At the same time, we recognize that the better response to the father's work request would be to say an honest "yes" followed by a good day of work in the vineyard.

From this perspective, we can think of the Gospel as a call to authentic Christian discipleship, which is energized by a fruitful combination of words and deeds. We become more credible Christians when we put our faith into action and when our verbal commitment to Christ manifests itself in everyday life.

Christ is our prime model of authentic human life. He lived what he taught, which contributed to his amazing impact on people. Paul's letter to the Philippians encourages us to have the same attitude found in Christ Jesus, who obediently humbled himself to the point of death, even death on a cross (see Philippians 2: 8). This remarkable act of selfless obedience forever reinforces and intensifies his command to love God wholeheartedly and do God's will on earth. The example of Jesus calls us to a more authentic Christian life.

We can imagine disciples of Christ making conscious efforts to match words and deeds. A couple in a troubled marriage work their way through their problems in fidelity to their marriage vows. A priest writes down the names of people who requested his prayers so that he will remember them at Mass. A father cuts down on his drinking so he can be a more authentic example of moderation to his teenage son. On Sundays, a single woman looks for one concrete way she can put the message of the liturgy into practice at work. A wife begins to treat her husband with greater kindness when she realizes that she has excluded him from her commitment to love others.

As we have learned anew from the example of Pope Francis, authentic Christian discipleship makes a positive impact on a world threatened by cynicism. Closing the gap between words and deeds is one way of demonstrating the intrinsic power of the Gospel of Jesus Christ.

How can I become a more credible witness to Christ?

141. How seriously do I take the law of love?

To test Jesus, a Pharisaic scholar asks him which of the recognized 613 laws is the greatest. Avoiding the then-current disputes on this question, Jesus identifies the greatest and first commandment: "You shall love the Lord your God with all your heart, and with all your soul, and with all your mind"—a familiar passage from Deuteronomy 6: 5, recited each day by observant Jews. Quoting Leviticus 18: 19, Jesus then adds a second like it: "You shall love your neighbor as yourself" (Matthew 22: 34-40).

In this brilliant move, Jesus combined two elements of his Jewish religious heritage into a lofty ideal that has guided and energized Christian discipleship ever since. His disciples understood that the two unified commands had to be kept together in order to avoid a deceitful contradiction: those who say they love God and hate their neighbor are liars. In Christ's teaching, we can also hear a call to develop a healthier self-love and more positive self-image that enables us to love God and neighbor more fully and effectively. In addition, the law of love is an ongoing challenge to self-righteousness and a powerful catalyst for spiritual growth.

The command to love God and neighbor does not function like other laws. We can examine our conscience at the end of a day and find that we have totally kept the command against stealing, murder, and adultery, yet we can never say we have completely fulfilled the law of love. The influential theologian Karl Rahner famously noted that love is true to itself only if it is prepared to give more tomorrow than today. We can never say that we have become perfect, that we have loved God as wholeheartedly as possible, that we have done all we can to love our neighbor. Christ's law of love not only precludes a prideful self-satisfaction but also serves as an ongoing invitation to take the next step forward on the spiritual journey.

We can envision Christians responding positively to today's Gospel. A man who prides himself on never missing Mass decides he has to get rid of his prejudice against minorities. A mother of three recognizes that she must improve her self-image in order to be a more loving parent. A senior citizen starts doing fifteen minutes of meditation twice a week in order to deepen his relationship with God. A teacher joins Bread for the World, which lobbies Congress on behalf of the hungry, in order to multiply her efforts to help the needy.

> What concrete step could I take to respond more fully to Christ's law of love?

142. Do I have escapist tendencies?

At the end of his Gospel, Matthew reports that the risen Christ appeared to his disciples on a mountain in Galilee, commissioning them to make disciples of all nations by baptizing them and teaching them all that he had commanded them. The passage concludes with a promise: "And remember, I am with you always, to the end of the age" (Matthew 28: 16-20). As baptized Christians today, we live under the missionary mandate of the Gospel. Our task is to promote the cause of Christ, to share in his mission to the world, to put forth our best effort to spread the kingdom.

Luke's version of the Ascension directs our attention to one of the temptations we face in carrying out our missionary vocation. After Jesus was lifted up before his disciples and disappeared in a cloud, the angels said to the apostles: "Men of Galilee, why do you stand looking up toward heaven?" (Acts 1:11).

Let us reflect on "looking up toward heaven" as a metaphor suggesting the common temptation to escape from the real challenges of our everyday life on this earth. One form of this escapism is to rely totally on God to solve human problems while failing to do our part to deal with them. For example, an alcoholic prays regularly to her higher power for help with her addiction, but does not attend AA meetings; a couple in a troubled marriage continue to attend Mass regularly hoping for divine intervention but resist seeking professional assistance; a high school teacher prays every day for her students but does little to stay up to date in her field; a priest does not prepare his Sunday homilies but relies on the Spirit for inspiration (which, incidentally, often makes the Holy Spirit look inept). We can all probably find such escapist tendencies, sometimes quite subtle and sometimes not, in our own lives.

Mindful of this temptation, we hear the Gospel calling us to participate in the mission of Christ which includes concrete action promoting human development. The ascended Lord, who no longer walks this earth, sends the Holy Spirit, empowering us to do our part in spreading God's reign in the world. As the traditional wisdom puts it: we should pray like everything depends on God and act like everything depends on us. Doing our part to carry on the work of Christ involves us in challenging situations that require hard work, careful planning, prudent decisions, and persevering efforts. An Ascension spirituality calls us to personal conversion by making us more attentive to the signs of the times; more understanding of the struggle between grace and sin; more reasonable about options for good; more responsible for spreading the reign of God.

To cooperate with God's grace, persons with a drinking problem might have to find a new circle of friends, start exercising during stressful times of the day, keep alcohol out of the house, and work a twelve-step program; a couple not happy with their marriage might do a Marriage Encounter, plan a weekly date night, set aside time to discuss feelings, and see a counselor; a teacher trying to stay current in her field might take an online course, read a book, attend a workshop, and consult with colleagues; a priest or deacon who comes to realize the importance of preparation for preaching might start on Monday, read a commentary, spend time in prayerful reflection, and participate in a faith sharing group.

How can I be more engaged in the mission of Christ?

143. Do I feel an obligation to serve others?

As Mark tells the story, Jesus travels from Nazareth to Judea where he is baptized by John in the Jordan River. Coming out of the water Jesus sees the Spirit descend upon him in the form of a dove and hears a voice from the heavens: "You are my Son, the Beloved; with you I am well pleased" (Mark 1: 9-11). Thus Jesus receives affirmation as Son of God and is anointed by the Spirit as the Suffering Servant portrayed by Isaiah, who will bring forth justice to the nations—opening the eyes of the blind and liberating the captives. Guided by the Spirit, Jesus carried out his public mission by going about doing good and healing all those oppressed by the devil.

The good news is that Christ shares his Spirit with us so that we can participate in his enlightening and liberating mission. Through our baptism, we are called to build up the Body of Christ and to spread his kingdom in the world.

Following the example of Christ, the Suffering Servant, we can live out our baptismal vocation by turning the crosses of life into opportunities to help others. An older couple, who successfully worked their way through serious problems in their marriage, now shares their experience with young couples in the parish marriage preparation program. A middle-age man, who was unemployed for a year before finding a good job, volunteers his time to help others in similar circumstances. A woman, who has survived breast cancer, is a big support to friends diagnosed with this disease. A high school teacher, who escaped from the drug culture many years ago, spends extra time helping students say "no" to drugs. A woman, who worked hard over several years to develop a spirituality that increased her self-esteem, facilitates a small group interested in spiritual growth.

> How can I live out my baptismal call to a life of service more effectively?

144. How can I help the poor?

I was hungry and you gave me food. Lord, when did we do that? When you did it for one of the least of the members of my family, you did it for me. This paraphrase from the Gospel of Matthew (Matthew 25:31-46) suggests that Christ, who lived not in royal luxury but as a poor Galilean peasant, identifies himself with his disciples in need and rewards those who do concrete acts of charity for his brothers and sisters. In a final performance review at the last judgment, we will be judged not by how many Masses we attended but by the way we responded to those in need.

One effective way of helping the needy is provided by the Catholic Campaign for Human Development (CCHD), established in 1970 by the U. S. Catholic bishops, to educate us on the problems of poverty in our country and to provide financial assistance for community-based self-help programs for the poor.

Consider these personal statements by individuals in favor of CCHD. A former inmate: "When I got out of prison, I doubted I could find employment, but a small business in Chicago that produces hand lotions gave me a job and taught me work skills that helped me get an even better job. Blessings on CCHD for helping to fund that program, which has helped many ex-offenders like me." A parishioner: "Every year I look forward to the Sunday before Thanksgiving because my pastor preaches on social justice and we take up a collection to help the poor." A grandmother: "For over forty years I have contributed to CCHD at least a couple times a year because it gives the poor not a handout but a hand up so they can escape the hellish circle of poverty." An affluent man: "I live in the suburbs and seldom encounter any poor people, so I appreciate the yearly effort of CCHD to put a human face on those living below the government poverty line." A senior citizen: "For many years, I felt overwhelmed by the problem of poverty and guilty for not doing more, but contributing to CCHD makes me feel like I am doing something constructive to help." A liberal

Catholic: "Having often been critical of the American bishops, I am glad to applaud them for starting and maintaining CCHD." A collegian: "Despite all the bad publicity directed at the Church, CCHD makes me proud to be a Catholic." A teacher: "CCHD reinforces my conviction that Catholic Social Teaching provides a great framework for responding to contemporary social problems." A conservative Catholic: "For a number of years, I resented CCHD Sunday because it disturbed my prayer time with God, but our pastor kept making the point that love of God must lead to love of neighbor, and now I am a big supporter of the campaign." A sister: "CCHD reminds me to pray for the poor in the city." A business woman: "I investigate the charities that ask for my help and am convinced that CCHD is most effective in helping the poor, so I make it my largest charitable contribution."

> What do I know and like about CCHD, and how can I increase my efforts to empower the poor in my community?

145. Am I tempted to self-righteousness or moral minimalism?

In Matthew's Sermon on the Mount, Jesus challenges our legalistic tendencies and puts before us a series of extremely high ideals (Matthew 5: 38-48). He wants us to love not only our friends who love us but also our enemies who hurt us. As followers of Jesus, we are to turn the other cheek and go the extra mile. The passage ends with the Lord calling us to be perfect "as our heavenly Father is perfect."

It is easy to dismiss the high idealism of the Gospel as impractical in the real world. We feel it might make sense for people living in a monastery or convent, but not for ordinary Christians faced with the give and take of everyday life. A more constructive response to the Gospel, however, is to see it as a challenge to minimalism and encouragement to keep striving for high ideals. Minimalism takes various forms: reducing the Christian life to avoiding serious sins; settling for mediocrity in relationships; limiting the call to holiness to a privileged few; doing just enough good to maintain respectability in the eyes of others; feeling self-righteous about personal development and achievements.

The Sermon on the Mount, however, does not prescribe ethical laws that can be obeyed only by a select few. Rather, it presents spiritual ideals—fully attainable by no one of us—that call all Christians to pursue perfection with calm assurance that our limited efforts are blessed and worthwhile. This approach leaves no room for self-righteousness, but it does open space for continuing efforts and lifelong spiritual growth.

We can imagine Christians who have responded positively to the high idealism of the Sermon on the Mount. A senior citizen who has said morning and night prayers almost every day since childhood, added fifteen minutes of Ignatian meditation to his daily prayer routine. A collegian who got average grades with little effort started to work harder and gets higher grades. A couple who settled for a mediocre marriage for decades agreed to do a Marriage Encounter weekend and now enjoy a more satisfying relationship. A middle-level manager who never caused any trouble at work decided to be a more positive presence by paying colleagues honest compliments. A citizen who voted regularly only to meet her civic responsibility committed herself to vote more intelligently by studying the candidates and issues before casting her ballot. A husband who often told his children to respect their mother reinforced his message by treating his wife with greater affection, understanding, and care. When Christ tells us to "go the extra mile," the proper response is not benign neglect but an honest effort to take the next constructive step.

In what specific way could I go the extra mile for Christ?

146. Am I too attached to money?

In the United States, there is a growing consumerist mentality that places a high value on having material things. The well-publicized lifestyle of the rich and famous fosters dreams of sharing in their glamorous world. Consumerism presumes that money can buy whatever we desire and that accumulating material possessions brings happiness. This mentality tends to see everything as a commodity that can be bought—even love, respect, and affection. It judges people successful according to how much money they make and what they can afford to buy. In a process called "branding," the world of advertising creates the illusion that buying only certain expensive items by specific companies can really qualify a person as having "made it."

Matthew's Gospel provides a striking challenge to the consumerist mentality. Jesus says to us: "You cannot serve God and wealth" (Matthew 6: 24-34). In other words, we cannot make money, wealth, and material possessions into an ultimate concern that rivals our commitment to God. Jesus goes on: "But strive first for the kingdom of God and his righteousness." Our top priority must be contributing to the establishment of love, justice, and peace in the world—not accumulating material possessions. Far from advocating a negative attitude toward material goods, like food and clothes, Jesus implies that eyes of faith can see these things as gifts from God who provides for our earthly needs. If we maintain the reign of God as our ultimate concern, then earthly goods can play their proper role in our lives, satisfying our physical needs and even nourishing our spirit.

Not many Christians would admit a wholehearted embrace of extreme consumerism. We could all benefit, however, from an honest examination of subtle ways this mentality has invaded our psyche. A man secretly harbors the conviction that most poor people in the United States are either lazy or immoral. A woman is envious of her neighbor who takes lavish vacations twice a year.

A young couple believes they will be happier if they can just afford more luxury items. A middle-class manager buys expensive brand name clothes in order to impress friends.

We can imagine persons making conscious decisions to resist consumerism and follow Gospel ideals. A woman who loves to dress fashionably decides to limit the number of new shoes she buys each year and to donate the money saved to the United Way. A grandfather decides to curtail his gambling on the horses so he can help his granddaughter go to college. In making their weekly budget, a couple decides to begin by setting aside additional money for the collection at Sunday Mass. A man decides to spend less time worrying about his stock portfolio and spend more time in prayerful reflection.

Given the immense influence of consumerism in our culture and the subtle ways it can invade our consciousness, we Christians are wise to make conscious decisions to serve God and not mammon.

> What could I do to resist the glamour of consumerism?

147. What extra baggage am I carrying?

In Mark's Gospel, Jesus sends out the Twelve, two by two, to preach repentance, to cast out demons, and to cure the sick. He instructs them to take nothing for the journey, except a staff and sandals—no bread, bag, money or extra tunic (Mark 6: 7-13). Jesus is commissioning his inner circle of disciples to participate in his preaching and healing ministry. They are to travel light, relying not on material goods but on the authority and power of their Lord.

We can hear this passage from Mark as a reminder that we are called to share in the ministry of Christ as were the Twelve. Our challenge is to live the Gospel in our own setting, to be a force for good in society, to help humanize culture, to spread the reign of God in our family circle and at our work site.

Christ's instruction to travel lightly on the journey of discipleship applies to us as well. It prompts reflection not on sandals and cloaks but on personal baggage that impedes our Christian witness: excessive worldly concerns that dominate attention; doubts about faith that weaken commitment; guilt feelings that siphon off energy; pride that supersedes reliance on God's grace. It is helpful to name the specific baggage that restricts our discipleship, while relying on Christ to lighten our burdens.

We can envision individuals, once burdened by baggage of various sorts, travelling lighter and living as better Christians. A wife feeling guilty about ignoring her husband's sexual desires went to confession, felt the burden of guilt lifted, and found herself more responsive to his initiatives. A middle-age man in the habit of spending a lot of money on clothes and toys came to realize that having so much stuff is more burdensome than satisfying and decided to simplify his lifestyle by devoting more time and energy to his family and friends. A young woman, raped by an acquaintance during her senior year in college, which left her weighed down with depression, sought professional help that enabled her to heal emotionally and experience life as less burdensome and more joyful.

> How could I travel lighter and be a more effective disciple of Christ?

148. Am I really aware of my gifts and talents?

Matthew tells us that Jesus and the disciples are faced with the problem of feeding a large crowd, 5,000 men plus women and children who have followed him to a deserted place (Matthew 14: 13-21), where he had gone to grieve the death of John the Baptist.

Instead, he spends the day preaching and curing their sick. The disciples, convinced that they did not have enough food for so many, propose that Jesus dismiss the crowd so they can go and buy food in the nearby villages. By way of contrast, Jesus concentrates on what they do have: five loaves and two fish. He thanks God for these gifts, breaks the loaves and divides the fish, and has the disciples share them with the crowd, who eat and are satisfied, leaving twelve wicker baskets of fragments.

This miracle of the feeding of the multitude, reported six times in the Gospels, suggests the power of Christ to feed human hungers and invites reflection on the difference between the approach of Jesus and that of his disciples. Christ, who satisfied the physical hunger of the large crowd, also nourishes us today as we deal with various human hungers, including the longing for personal fulfillment, loving relationships, healthy families, significant work, authentic community, and spiritual growth. In pursuing these goods, "the go and buy" strategy of the disciples is notoriously ineffective. We cannot buy love and happiness. The strategy Jesus used to feed the multitude is more promising: identify what we do have, thank God for these gifts, and share them with others—which does not diminish the things we have but multiplies them.

Let us consider some applications of the Lord's approach. A married couple has not been blessed with the children they wanted and expected. Instead of dwelling on this misfortune, they thank God for the love they share and commit themselves to various civic projects that help vitalize the community. A single man, who would like to be married, is grateful to God for his fulfilling career and uses his work experience to benefit the parish finance council. A woman who had to quit the job she loved as a social worker because of health problems does not complain but spends long hours praying for people in need. A retired truck driver, who no longer experiences the sensible consolation in private prayer he once enjoyed, continues to participate wholeheartedly in Sunday liturgy, opening himself to the possibility of a still deeper spiritual life.

We can interpret today's Gospel miracle as an invitation to concentrate more on blessings we have received than on things we don't have. Thanking God for these personal gifts prompts us to share them with others, confident that they are not exhausted in the process but are multiplied by Christ's amazing power.

> What gifts have I received from God and how can I share them with others?

149. Do I see myself participating in the mission of Christ?

Matthew tells us Jesus experienced a deep visceral compassion for the crowds who feel troubled and abandoned, like sheep without a shepherd (Matthew 9: 36-10: 8). In response, after advising prayer to God to send laborers for the harvest, he himself sends the twelve apostles to proclaim that the kingdom of heaven is at hand, not to the Gentiles and Samaritans, but to the lost sheep of the house of Israel. Giving them authority over unclean spirits, he tells them to cure the sick, raise the dead, cleanse lepers and drive out demons. Jesus completes his instructions to the twelve with a reminder: "You received without payment; give without payment."

The Gospel serves as a reminder to all Christians that we are called to share in the mission of Christ. Like the twelve apostles, we are empowered by the Lord to continue his work of proclaiming and extending the reign of God; unlike the twelve our mission is not restricted to fellow believers but extends to all we encounter on the journey. As Vatican II taught us, we are all called to holiness and we are all responsible for spreading the kingdom in the world. Pope Francis wants all of us to have a missionary mentality that prompts us to serve others and to care for the earth. Prayer is essential to living our missionary vocation and persevering in our efforts to humanize the world. We have received the gift of faith as a free gift, at no cost, and we should be ready to share its fruits generously, at no cost, with others.

Christians today find strength and guidance in meeting those everyday responsibilities when they see themselves as sent by Christ to share in his mission. Grandparents forced by circumstances to raise their daughter's child have persevered in this demanding task by thinking of their situation as a second vocation. Despite increasing danger, a police officer goes on duty every day to carry out his calling to protect the citizens in his town. A religious education director who serves her parish wisely and generously, sees her work not as a job but as a vocation. A father of three kids, who works two jobs to support his family, reminds himself on especially fatiguing days that he can count on the Lord's assistance.

> What next step could I take to share more fully in the mission of Christ?

150. How can I promote peace?

Luke tells us that Jesus appointed seventy others and sent them in pairs to the towns and places he intended to visit. He sent them "like lambs into the midst of wolves," instructing them to travel lightly, no purse, no bag, and no sandals. They are to bring peace to households, cure the sick and proclaim that the kingdom of God is near (Luke 10: 1-12). Luke goes on to inform us that the seventy returned rejoicing and said, "Lord, in your name even the demons submit to us!" Jesus responded that they should rejoice not because of their power over spirits, but because their "names are written in heaven" (Luke 10: 17-20).

As baptized Christians, we too are sent by Christ to share in his mission. We are called to help spread the Kingdom of God, to bring peace to our corner of the world. In that task, we encounter wolves, demonic forces that tear at the fiber of divine peace. The good news, as the seventy-two discovered, is that Christ is more powerful than all the dark forces. His peace will ultimately prevail over Satan and the evil spirits.

We all know Christians who have cooperated with Christ in bringing peace to their circles of influence. A father mediated an ongoing dispute between his wife and their teenage daughter by getting them to talk together to the pastor of their parish. A small business owner overcame some hard feelings among her employees by periodically providing free social events where they could have fun and interact on a personal basis. A pastor healed a split in his parish over renovation of the church by arranging a series of open meetings where both sides could freely express their views on various aspects of the issue.

We could also apply to ourselves the advice of Jesus to travel lightly and shed excess baggage as we carry on our daily tasks of sharing in his mission. Some examples. An overweight woman, who followed a regimen of regular exercise and healthy eating, lost weight and gained more energy for her responsibilities as a wife and mother. A man subject to periodic irrational outbursts of anger got professional help and became a much more effective peacemaker at work and in the family setting. A young woman burdened by negative images of an angry God, made a retreat which enabled her to develop a more positive notion of a God slow to anger and rich in kindness. A former Catholic, divorced and remarried, who was for years estranged from the Church, read the exhortation of Pope Francis on the family which lifted a burden of guilt and brought him back to the Church.

What specific action could I take to promote peace?

151. Do I strive for the high idealism of the beatitudes?

Luke's version of the beatitudes has a large crowd assembled on a plain with Jesus addressing his disciples: "Blessed are you who are poor, for yours is the kingdom of God." Following a similar pattern of reversal, Jesus goes on to declare blessed the hungry, who will be filled; those weeping, who will laugh; and the persecuted, who will enjoy a great reward in heaven (Luke 6: 20-26).

The Gospel challenges standard ways of seeing life in this world. As events unfold in real time, something much deeper is happening; the reign of God is being established and extended. This reign (or kingdom) embodies God's will for the world. God's ways are not our ways. Kingdom ideals challenge worldly wisdom. Christians experience a tension between Gospel teachings and secular values. For being faithful to the cause of God, Jesus himself was persecuted to the point of death on the cross, which issued for him in a new glorified life. Jesus embodies and exemplifies the pattern of reversal in Luke's beatitudes.

As Christians we are to learn from the example of Jesus as well as his teaching on the beatitudes. We cannot simply accept the ways of the world as normative. Our faith instructs us to look deeper for signs of the kingdom and work harder to extend its influence. Luke's beatitudes do not promise that the poor will get rich or that the persecuted will have an easy life. They do suggest that those who suffer can count on God's grace abundantly available to them now.

For followers of Jesus, there is always an obligation to do all we can to alleviate suffering, to assist the needy, to empower the marginalized, to overcome injustice, to fight systemic evils. We cannot use the first beatitude, blessed are the poor, for example, to absolve ourselves of responsibility to reduce poverty. On the contrary, it reminds us that the poor have dignity and worth, that they have much to teach others, and that they deserve an opportunity to escape the hellish circle of poverty.

We can imagine positive responses to Luke's distinctive version of the beatitudes. A single mother living below the poverty line while raising three children is moved to take a free seminar on improving job skills, which leads her to a better paying job and a greater sense of self-worth. A high school senior well respected as a football star comes to the defense of a fellow student being bullied and effectively ends the problem by befriending the victim. A parishioner gets her parish to set up a food distribution program to feed the hungry in the neighborhood. A clinical psychologist, who grew spiritually when grieving the loss of his wife, begins offering free grief counseling to those who cannot afford it.

> What could I do to help empower the poor?

152. Do I see myself living a Christian vocation?

John's Gospel tells the story of how Andrew and his brother Simon became followers of Jesus (John 1: 35-42). Andrew, a disciple of John the Baptist, follows Jesus after John points him out as the Lamb of God. At the invitation of Jesus, Andrew spends a day with him. Convinced by this brief encounter that Jesus is the Messiah, Andrew brings his brother Simon to Jesus, who looks at Simon and says, "You are to be called Cephas," which is translated Peter.

The interesting personal dynamics of the story prompt reflection on the people who have influenced our lives as Christian disciples: grandparents, parents, siblings, friends, spouses, sisters, priests, saints. The eyes of faith discern a call from Christ himself working through all the good people who have influenced the direction of our lives.

As Vatican II has taught us, we all have a vocation to follow Christ and participate in his mission to spread the reign of God in the world. By virtue of our baptism, we are called to use our distinct talents and gifts in the great cause of creating a community of justice and peace, where human beings can flourish. We live out our Christian vocation in all the ordinary activities of life: going to school, pursuing a career, founding a family, raising children, maintaining friendships, working hard, contributing to civic life, participating in parish life, enjoying leisure activities, and meeting daily responsibilities. The whole range of human activities, often routine and sometimes tedious, take on deeper meaning when viewed from the perspective of our baptismal vocation to share in Christ's mission and cause.

Some examples: a husband is much happier in his marriage when he recognizes his vocation to help his wife grow spiritually; a licensed practical nurse working with the elderly finds more meaning in her work when she sees herself living the Christian vocation to serve people in need; a young man choosing a career path feels less stress when he considers all of his options as opportunities to live out his fundamental Christian vocation; a stay-at-home mother feels more confident about her choice when she thinks of it as a vocation with intrinsic value; a homebound grandmother, who can no longer care for her family, continues her maternal vocation by spending time each day praying for the specific needs of her children and grandchildren.

> What specific step could I take to be more faithful to my Christian vocation?

153. What could I do to foster Christian unity?

Matthew tells the story of the initial efforts of Jesus to found a community of followers who would respond to his essential message, "Repent, for the kingdom of heaven has come near" (Matthew 4: 17-22). He called Peter and his brother Andrew, and they left their fishing business and followed him. Likewise, the Zebedee brothers, James and John, heard the call of Jesus, left their father and their boat and followed their new Master. We know that Jesus continued to gather followers, instruct them, and form them into a community which would carry on his mission after his death and resurrection.

However, divisions plagued the Jesus movement from its early days as, for example, rivalries developed in Corinth. Two thousand years later, the Christian world is still suffering from divisions that thwart Christ's will and weaken our witness in the world. The second millennium was a disaster for the cause of Christian unity. In 1054, the Christian East and Christian West officially excommunicated each other, leaving us with a continuing split between Orthodox Christians and Roman Catholics. The Protestant Reformation in the 16th century brought further fragmentation into the Christian world, resulting in an enduring division between Catholics and a vast variety of Protestant denominations. Furthermore, within the Catholic community today, we have the problem of polarization, which leads to sharp and sometimes acrimonious disputes between groups often identified as "liberals" or "conservatives."

A healthy response to divisions among Christians is to focus on Christ and his central message. At the Last Supper, Jesus prayed that his followers would stay united and that there would be one flock and one shepherd, so that the world might believe in him. Division weakens Christian witness; unity honors the will of Christ. The Church functions most effectively when it follows the more excellent way of love, which is patient, kind, and persevering. The community of faith is held together by the common belief in Christ, who died for our sins, was buried, and was raised on the third day. The path to Christian unity is marked by greater fidelity to Christ, crucified and risen, who taught us by word and example to love God and neighbor.

Pope Francis has revitalized a faltering ecumenical movement by focusing on Christ and his central message of love. A Russian Orthodox bishop applauded the pope's emphasis on "service to the poor" as a good starting point for Roman Catholic and Russian Orthodox Churches to find new ways to work together. After meeting with Pope Francis in Rome, the Archbishop of Canterbury spoke of their shared commitment to offer the love of Christ to the poor and marginalized. Leaders of the World Council of Churches praised the pope's Apostolic Exhortation, *The Joy of the Gospel*, as a promising basis for dialogue and collaboration. At the grassroots level, Pope Francis has been a source of inspiration and hope for many ordinary Christians, Protestant as well as Catholic, by the exemplary way he lives the simple Gospel message. He reminds all of us that we can contribute to the cause of Christian unity by a personal conversion of heart that deepens our commitment to Christ and his core message of forgiveness and reconciliation.

> What can I learn from Pope Francis on participating in the ecumenical movement?

154. Do I recognize my responsibility to spread the Kingdom in the world?

In John's Gospel, Jesus declares: "Believe in God, believe also in me (John 14: 1-14). Those who do believe in Jesus and his intimate relationship with the Father will do the works Jesus did. They will share in his mission to the world. The first letter of Peter grounds and specifies this Gospel truth: "But you are a chosen race, a royal priesthood, a holy nation, God's own people" (Peter 2:9) The Second Vatican Council referred to this verse in developing its teaching on the Church as the People of God. The Council reminds us that all Christians, by virtue of our baptism, share in the priesthood of Christ. All Christians are called to holiness and are co-responsible for building up the Body of Christ and spreading his kingdom in the world.

In the half century since Vatican II, we have made tremendous strides in increasing lay involvement in the internal life of the church. We have many dedicated people serving as lectors, Eucharistic ministers, religious education directors, pastoral administrators, music ministers, and many more who work to build up the Body of Christ.

We have not done as well on the responsibility of all the baptized to spread the kingdom in the world. Our community still suffers from an unfortunate disconnect between liturgy and life, between what we proclaim at Mass and what we do in our everyday activities. Some who attend Mass regularly resist the application of the Gospel to the challenges we face in the economic and political realms. Others fail to make any explicit connections between their faith and the good they do in everyday life. For many, the rich body of Catholic social teaching remains a well-kept secret.

During his pontificate, Pope Francis has made a great effort to revive the People of God image of the Church, with its emphasis on the baptismal priesthood. Let us envision developments in a parish that follows his lead. Many parishioners do a better job of relating the Sunday liturgy to everyday life in the world. In his preaching, the pastor is more attentive to relating the scripture readings to the real concerns of the congregation. More parishioners look to their Christian faith for guidance in making decisions about economic and political issues. The parish initiates a variety of educational opportunities to learn more about Catholic social teaching while expanding its Christian service projects. More members of the parish turn to their faith for motivation in meeting their responsibilities to their families, to their work, and their community. The annual parish blessing for liturgical ministers is expanded to include those working for justice and peace.

As a result of all these developments, the parish as a whole grows in its understanding of itself as a leaven in society, a force for good within the neighborhood, and a community of faith in the world dedicated to serving the common good.

As baptized members of the people of God, we all participate in the priesthood of Christ and share in his mission to spread the reign of God in the world. Pope Francis has blessed us with a marvelous opportunity to renew our commitment to this mission. Let us seize the moment.

> How could I participate more fully in the priesthood and mission of Christ?